"Read My Lips"

Classic Texas Political Quotes

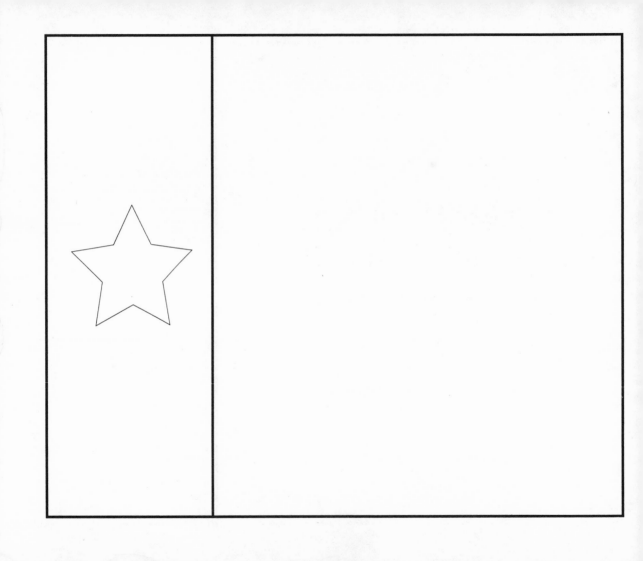

"Read My Lips"

Classic Texas Political Quotes

Kirk Dooley and Eben Price

Illustrations by Kent Gamble

Foreword by George W. Bush

Texas Tech University Press

This book was set in New Century Schoolbook and Tek-
ton and printed on acid-free paper that meets the guidelines for permanence and durability of the committee on
Production Guidelines for Book Longevity of the council on
Library Resources. ∞

Art by Kent Gamble
Manufactured in the United States of America.

Library of Congress Cataloging-in-Publication Data
    Dooley, Kirk.
        "Read my lips" : classic Texas political quotes / by Kirk Dooley
    and Eben Price ; illustrations by Kent Gamble.
            p.   cm.
        Includes index.
        ISBN 0-89672-350-X (paper)
        1. Texas—Politics and government—Quotations, maxims, etc.
    I. Price, Eben, 1955-   II. Title.
    F386.D65 1995
    976.4—dc20   95-3409
                                                   CIP

95 96 97 98 99 00 01 02 03 / 9 8 7 6 5 4 3 2 1

Texas Tech University Press
P. O. Box 41037
Lubbock, Texas 79409-1037 USA
1-800-832-4042

iv

Contents

V

Classic Texas Quotes

Kirk Dooley, Series Editor
Kent Gamble, Series Illustrator

"...'Til the Fat Lady Sings"
Classic Texas Sports Quotes
Alan Burton

"Read My Lips"
Classic Texas Political Quotes
Kirk Dooley and Eben Price

Foreword

Texans take their politics seriously, perhaps too seriously sometimes. Many Texans consider politics to be a contact sport; some, a blood sport. In our history, we've seen armed vigilantes evicting losing candidates from office, heard white hot rhetoric from the stump that evoked challenges to duels, and enough charges of stolen ballots and fraudulent election returns to make a big-city machine boss green with envy.

Texas political history was written by a colorful cast of characters. Few states have had such variety of those who held or sought public office.

Texas, of course, has more than its fair share of great leaders, too, men and women who left their mark on our state and country. And fortunately for the connoisseur of political speech, many of them were quick with a quip.

Some say the age of larger-than-life figures is drawing to a close. I hope not, for our state's political scene has been enlivened by their words. They've engaged and amused us, cast a bright light on our foibles, and, as Kirk Dooley and Eben Price have demonstrated in this collection of quotes, contributed much to the unique culture that's Texas.

Governor George W. Bush
Austin 1995

Preface

Democracy: an ideal form of government in which the people govern themselves. Elected representatives listen to the voice of the people, and they heed their instructions. These officials consider a job well done to be ample reward, and they seek no other compensation. Great issues of the day are debated openly and eloquently on the floor of the legislature. The governor and the courts work in harmony with the legislature to assure that government always does what is best for the peple.

Luckily, the world of Texas politics is nothing like that description, or else we wouldn't have been able to put this book together.

Indeed, it is the unapologetic departure from the ideal that gives Texas and its politicians their distinctive character. Most Texans wouldn't recognize (or perhaps even trust) a government that didn't prominently feature backroom deals, that "big bidness," and mudslinging. We have tried to capture some of that atmosphere, thanks

mainly to the words of the movers and shakers themselves, with the reactions of some concerned citizens thrown in for good measure.

Journalists have been the primary conduit for revealing Texas politicians to their constituents, and their mixture of fascination and skepticism has been our guiding principle in assembling these quotations. We owe a debt of gratitude to our high school journalism teacher, Reyburn Myers, in this regard. She once described the daily dilemma of a newspaper as being, "we don't make the news, and we don't print it all, either." In that spirit, if you read through this book and feel a quotation may be too outrageous, keep in mind two things: (1) we didn't say it; he or she did, and (2) we may have left out something even worse!

Kirk Dooley
Eben Price

To a couple of young Texans:

My daughter Maggie
   —Kirk Dooley

My son Robert
   —Eben Price

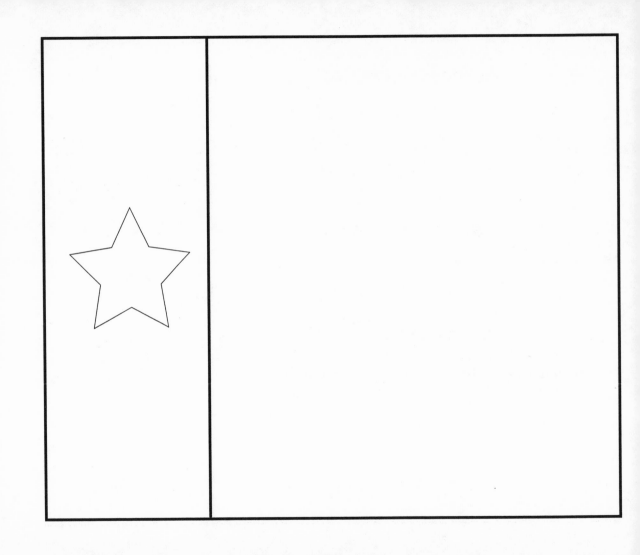

Acknowledgments

We are indebted to the following for providing much of the inspiration for this project: *Austin American-Statesman,* CBS, *D Magazine, The Dallas Morning News, Dallas Times Herald* (RIP), *Homesick Texan, Houston Chronicle, The Houston Post* (RIP), *Iconoclast* (RIP), *Texas Observer, Texas Lawyer, Texas Monthly, Texas State Gazette* (RIP), *Texas Weekly,* and *Ultra Magazine* (RIP).

We are also indebted to Charles Herring, Jr. and Walter Richter, the authors of the book *Don't Throw Feathers at Chickens,* published by Wordware Publishing Inc. in Plano, Texas. We recommend this book for our readers who enjoy the humor in Texas Politics.

xiii

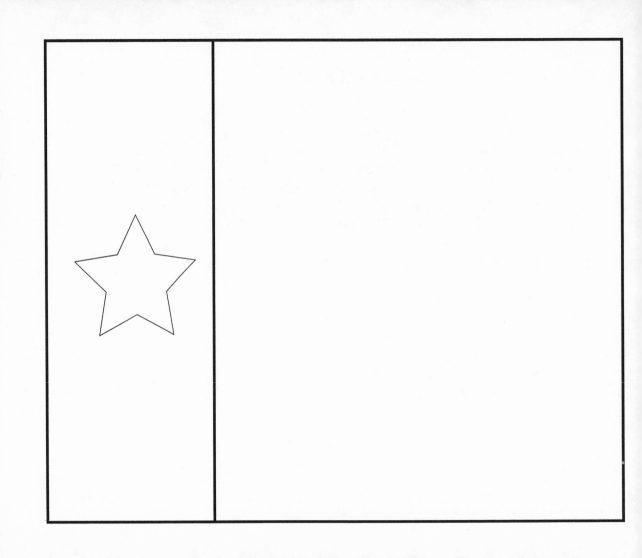

"Read My Lips"

Classic Texas Political Quotes

"ONE MAN WHO GIVES
NO QUARTER"
(No place but Texas)

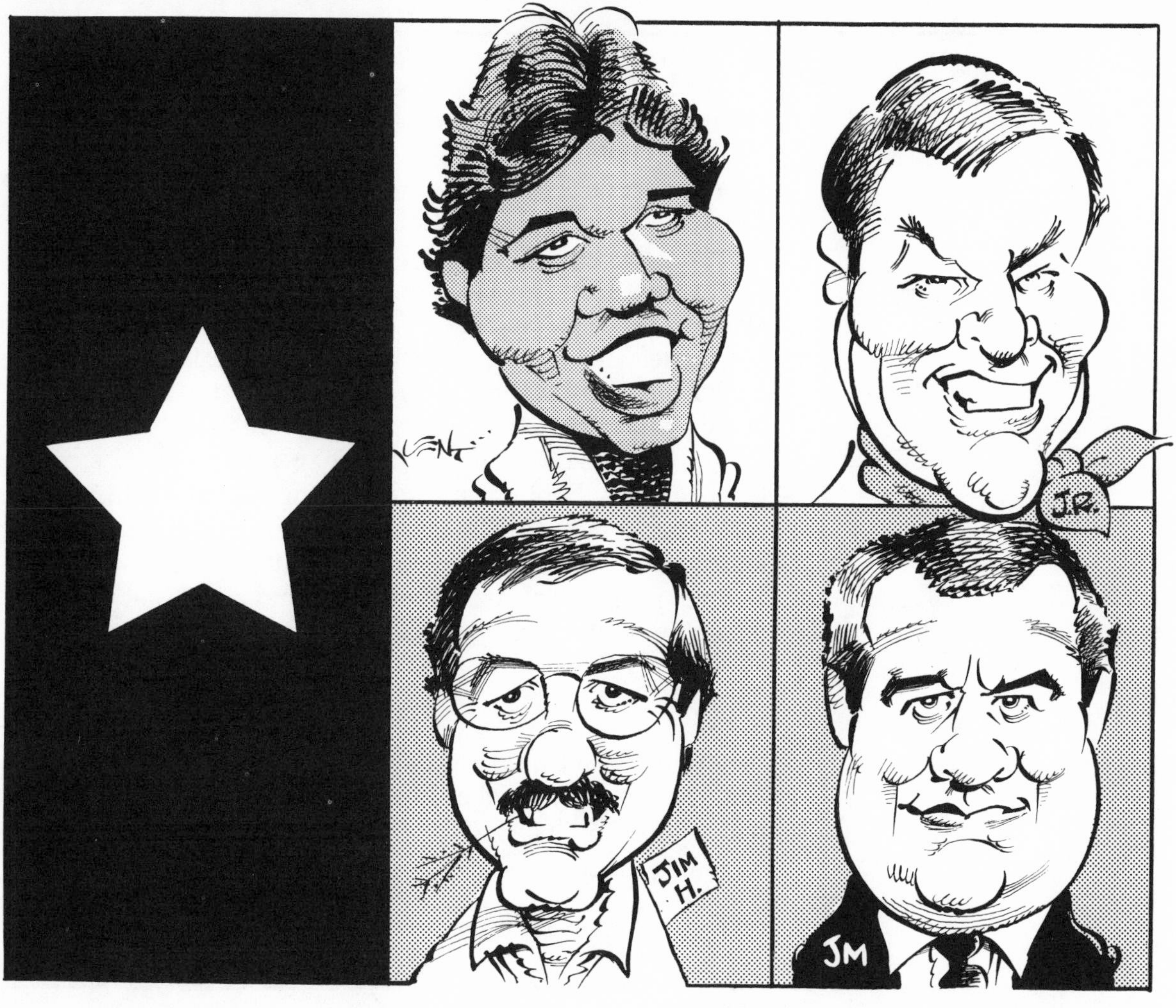
J.R.
JIM H.
JM

4

More than any other chapter in this book, the political quotes here in "One Man Who Gives No Quarter" reflect that unique spirit and Texas state of mind that you won't find in Oklahoma, New Jersey or any other foreign country.

The quotes in this chapter celebrate the popular slogan, "No place but Texas!"

Charles Herring, Jr., and Walter Richter, in their book *Don't Throw Feathers at Chickens,* retell the story by former Texas Supreme Court Justice Jack Pope. It seems that friends of former Attorney General R. L. Bobbitt enjoyed kidding him about his renowned frugality. The best quote came from the shoe shine man at the Driskill Hotel in Austin: "Mr. Bobbitt is the most courageous man I ever knew. He is one man who gives no quarter."

☆☆☆

"There are two things that every genuine, true American should have at his fingertips at all times: a gun and a Bible."

Concerned citizen and East Texan Lonnie Roberts, 1966,
in a letter to
The Dallas Morning News

"Texas—so big, so great, so considerate—to be one of the only places left in the world where it is legal to drive with a cold beer in the open. That is the preservation of positive legislation."

Actor Dan Aykroyd
Texas Is

☆ ☆ ☆

"Herman Brown was a businessman who wanted value for money spent. His relationships with politicians were measured by that criterion."

LBJ biographer Robert Caro, 1982
The Path to Power

☆ ☆ ☆

"I went directly to the Dallas Public Library and read the complete works of A. C. Greene, because A. C. Greene wrote all the books in the Dallas Public Library, starting with *Famous Drunk Indians That Visited Dallas in the 1860s and Got Killed with Muskets*, continuing right on through *Dallas in the Eighties: Gimme Some Money.*"

Texas-based "drive-in movie critic" Joe Bob Briggs, 1988,
explaining his first step in solving the John F. Kennedy assassination
A Guide to Western Civilization, or My Story

5

6

"In Texas, a political speech is sometimes referred to as a longhorn: one that makes two good points, but they are a long way apart and have a lot of bull in between."

Observation recorded by Herring and Richter
Don't Throw Feathers at Chickens

☆ ☆ ☆

"She [Charlotte Mayes] is running as a white woman who represents the worst of white power."

Dallas city councilwoman Diane Ragsdale, who was defeated by her opponent, Charlotte Mayes—both women are black.
D Magazine, January 1992

☆ ☆ ☆

"I am an optimist. If I ever quit being an optimist, I guess I'll become a Republican."

Senator Ray Farabee of Wichita Falls
Texas Weekly, December 9, 1985

"I believe that women have a capacity for understanding and compassion which a man structurally does not have, because he cannot have it. He's just incapable of it."

Former U. S. Representative Barbara Jordan to an Austin Women's Conference
Texas Monthly, January 1992

☆ ☆ ☆

"I can tell you two things about Johnny. The first is, he has never been in the Texas Penitentiary. The second is, I don't know why."

Texas humorist John Henry Faulk, on a friend who had just introduced him to a group.
Don't Throw Feathers at Chickens

☆ ☆ ☆

"I appreciate your welcome. As the cow said to the Amarillo farmer, 'Thank you for a warm hand on a cold day.'"

Classic Texas campaign trail opener with rural audiences
Don't Throw Feathers at Chickens

"If you own an S&L in Texas, you sleep like a baby—you wake up every three hours and cry."

Texas savings and loan owner John Selman
Texas Weekly, October 10, 1988

☆ ☆ ☆

"How do you get a [Texas] banker out of a tree? You cut the rope."

Texas political financier Jess Hay
Texas Weekly, February 19, 1988

☆ ☆ ☆

Democracy: "The art of saying 'nice doggie, nice doggie' until you can find a rock."

Texas political observer Wynn Catlin
Don't Throw Feathers at Chickens

☆ ☆ ☆

"In Texas, we do not hold high expectations from the office; it's mostly been occupied by crooks, dorks and the comatose."

Texas-based political columnist and humorist Molly Ivins, on the governor's office in Texas
Molly Ivins Can't Say That, Can She?

"If they're eligible to vote, they ought to be eligible to be appointed to a commission."

Agriculture Commissioner John White, when ribbed by a New Mexico official about Governor Dolph Briscoe's having appointed a dead man to a commission
Don't Throw Feathers at Chickens

☆ ☆ ☆

"Hell, there's no back door at the Alamo. That's why we had so many dead heroes."

Texas legislator Maury Maverick, Jr., responding to a request to allow John F. Kennedy to leave the Alamo through the back door to avoid a large crowd out front, 1960
Too Funny To Be President

☆ ☆ ☆

"Feller, if I was St. Peter, you wouldn't be in my district."

Unknown but quick-thinking Texas politician, responding to heckler at a political rally who taunted, "Mister, I wouldn't vote for you if you were St. Peter!"
Don't Throw Feathers at Chickens

9

10

"[Harley Schlanger, a LaRouchite] is a nutty, right-wing economist, and that gives me three months to practice before meeting Phil Gramm."

Hugh Parmer, during his primary race for U.S. Senate, about his primary opponent
Texas Weekly, March 12, 1990

☆ ☆ ☆

"In politics, a lie unanswered becomes truth within 24 hours."

Willie Brown, former Texan and longtime Speaker of California Assembly
Don't Throw Feathers at Chickens

☆ ☆ ☆

"Baptists are just like cats. You know they're doing it, but you just can't catch them at it."

Singer-songwriter Allen Damron, on Texans who drink beer
Texas: A Self Portrait

☆ ☆ ☆

"Everybody's somebody in Luckenbach."

Luckenbach "imagineer" Hondo Crouch
Hondo, My Father

"A pushy lady patriot stopped San Antonio Mayor Maury Maverick Sr. in the lobby of the St. Anthony Hotel and said, 'Someone told me the other day that you are a communist, but I didn't believe them.' Maverick shot back, 'Madam, somebody told me the other day that you are a whore, but I didn't believe them.'"

Lady Bird Johnson's White House Secretary Liz Carpenter tells this story about the Texas rawhide candor of the late Maury Maverick, Sr.
Don't Throw Feathers at Chickens

☆ ☆ ☆

"Join me in welcoming one of the best public officials this state has ever sent to California for treatment."

U.S. Representative Jake Pickle, introducing Bob Bullock at a Texas Women's Political Caucus benefit "roast"
Don't Throw Feathers at Chickens

☆ ☆ ☆

"Politics: The art of keeping as many balls as possible up in the air at one time—while protecting your own."

Political columnist Sam Attlesey
The Dallas Morning News

12

"Have you ever examined the word 'politics'? Poly means many and ticks means bloodsuckers."

Theresa Doyle, Libertarian
Texas Weekly, March 24, 1986

☆ ☆ ☆

"Politics is show biz for ugly people."

Political consultant Bill Miller
Don't Throw Feathers at Chickens

☆ ☆ ☆

"The women's rights movement is the most vicious, conniving, deceiving movement this country has ever seen next to communism."

Representative Larry Vick of Houston
Molly Ivins Can't Say That, Can She?

☆ ☆ ☆

Modern politics consists of "choosing between the disastrous and the unpalatable."

Economist John Kenneth Galbraith, during a lecture at the University of Texas
Don't Throw Feathers at Chickens

"The ability to wear a $10,000 dress and eat caviar in front of a baboon cage once a year doesn't necessarily mean you have the judgment to tell the citizens of Fort Worth what's good for them."

Fort Worth attorney Tim Evans, after the Fort Worth City Council voted to allow the zoo to expand—a controversial move championed by the city's social elite
Texas Monthly, January 1988

☆ ☆ ☆

"Republicans are so empty-headed, they wouldn't make a good landfill."

Agriculture Commissioner Jim Hightower
Don't Throw Feathers at Chickens

☆ ☆ ☆

"Real Texans do not use the word 'summer' as a verb."

Molly Ivins
Texas Monthly, November 1992

13

14

"They are satanic people. Either you are on God's side or Satan's."

Tarrant County Republican executive committee chairman Jim Ryan, on his resignation after the committee voted down his proposal to condemn the film *The Last Temptation of Christ*
Texas Monthly, January 1989

☆ ☆ ☆

"I'm not afraid to play anywhere. We played at Big G's in Round Rock."

Country music legend Willie Nelson, announcing the rescheduling of his Belfast, North Ireland concert, which had been canceled by his manager, who feared political violence
Texas Monthly, January 1989

☆ ☆ ☆

"I am not a member of any organized political party. I am a Democrat."

Humorist Will Rogers
Don't Throw Feathers at Chickens

"It was the white liberals who marched with me so I could play golf, go bowling, and try on clothes in downtown Odessa. Now I'm hearing there's something wrong with them, and instead, those people who tried to keep me out—the city officials, the sheriffs, the power brokers—they're my friends. I prefer to adhere to what Darrell Royal says, 'You dance with who brung ya.'"

Gary Bledsoe of the Texas State Conference of the NAACP
Texas Monthly, January 1992

☆ ☆ ☆

"The things you do for your kids."

Wanda Holloway, the mom who, caught up in the politics of Texas high school cheerleading, was charged with hiring a hit man to kill the mother of her daughter's cheerleading opponent before the election
Texas Monthly, January 1992

☆ ☆ ☆

"Advertising men and politicians are dangerous if they are separated. Together they are diabolical."

Political observer Phillip Adams
Don't Throw Feathers at Chickens

15

"What he does on his own time is up to him."

Bexar County Sheriff Harlon Copeland, on what he planned to do about a deputy who was charged with exposing himself to a child
Texas Monthly, January 1992

☆ ☆ ☆

"There are honest journalists like there are honest politicians. When bought, they stay bought."

Journalist Bill Moyers
Don't Throw Feathers at Chickens

☆ ☆ ☆

"Dad and I had breakfast this morning. We had a look at each other's speeches. He would have used mine, but he's not a lesbian. I would have used his, but I'm not a Republican."

Diane Mosbacher, daughter of Secretary of Commerce Robert Mosbacher
Texas Monthly, January 1992

☆ ☆ ☆

"If Strauss is the ultimate capitalist, then Bonnie and Clyde were the ultimate bankers."

Bill Moyers on Democratic Party power broker Robert Strauss
Texas Monthly, January 1992

16

"When I entered politics, I took the only downward turn you could take from journalism."

Jim Hightower
Don't Throw Feathers at Chickens

☆ ☆ ☆

"Give me somebody I know I don't like rather than a hypocrite who says he's for me when he's not."

Dallas-Fort Worth black journalist Bob Ray Sanders, on why he endorsed ex-Klansman David Duke in the Louisiana Governor's race
Texas Monthly, January 1992

☆ ☆ ☆

"The only difference between a pigeon and the American farmer today is that a pigeon can still make a deposit on a John Deere."

Jim Hightower
The Best of Texas

☆ ☆ ☆

"[They] are the kind of people that are just nearly a cult. They could wind up drinking poison Kool-Aid, like Jim Jones in Guyana."

Attorney General Jim Mattox, on the followers of his adversary Rev. W. N. Otwell
D Magazine, January 1987

17

18

"If a man's from Texas, he'll tell you. If he's not, why embarrass him by asking?"

Travel writer John Gunther
The Best of Texas

☆ ☆ ☆

"The Republicans [wore] $1,200 red, white and blue shoes, and gowns by Galanos and Yves St. Laurent. The homeless favored the layered look, topped by a street-chic wool cap, accessorized by mittens with the fingers worn out."

Molly Ivins, covering the Bush inauguration in 1989
D Magazine, January 1990

☆ ☆ ☆

"Sometimes when you get in a fight with a skunk, you can't tell who started it."

Texas politician Lloyd Doggett
The Best of Texas

"Oil rich boys . . . had a nice, sweet smile but when you finished meeting with them your socks were missing and you hadn't even noticed they'd taken your boots."

Actor (and native Texan) Larry Hagman
The Best of Texas

☆ ☆ ☆

"I understand he's arrogant and somewhat aggressive, and so, too, am I."

Dallas County Commissioner John Wiley Price, on talk-show host Morton Downey, Jr., who streamrollered Dallas County officials and won the right to broadcast his show from the "sniper's perch" overlooking Dealey Plaza. Price opposed the request.
D Magazine, January 1993

☆ ☆ ☆

"Sharing is the essence of teaching. It is, I have come to believe, the essence of civilization. The impulse to share turns from the mere pursuit of power and makes journalism a public service. It inspires art, builds cities, and spreads knowledge."

Bill Moyers
The Best of Texas

19

20

"That's like the Mayflower Madam calling Hester Prynne a slut."

Dallas County Democratic party chairman Ken Molberg, on U.S. Representative Dick Armey's comparison of the Democrats' long hold on Congress to Castro's dictatorship. Molberg noted that Armey had nineteen overdrafts of his own at the House bank.
D Magazine, January 1993

☆ ☆ ☆

"We have a reputation for never squeezing the last nickel out of a deal. My grandmother had an expression, 'Pigs get fat, and hogs get slaughtered.'"

Texas businessman Ray Hunt
The Best of Texas

☆ ☆ ☆

"My focus is not on selling more chickens, because when I face Jesus Christ on Judgment Day, He won't ask how many chickens I sold."

Texas businessman and political deal-maker Bo Pilgrim
Texas Monthly, September 1994

"Brotherhood doesn't come in a package. It is not a commodity to be taken down from the shelf with one hand. It is an accomplishment of soul-searching prayer and perseverance. . . . The spontaneous feeling of brotherhood is a mark of human maturity."

Publisher Oveta Culp Hobby
The Best of Texas

☆ ☆ ☆

"Manure is manure. It's hard to keep it from smelling."

Bo Pilgrim
Texas Monthly, September 1994

☆ ☆ ☆

"What does everyone want to see happen in our world today? They want justice. God knows there is so much injustice in our society today—people murdering somebody and getting out in two years— that the guilty suffer less than the victims. That's why people see Walker and say, 'Yeah, at least he'll take care of things.'"

Chuck Norris, star of "Walker, Texas Ranger"
Texas Monthly, April 1994

21

22

"[H. L.] Hunt gave capitalism a bad name not, goodness knows, by frenzies of extravagance, but by his eccentric understanding of public affairs, his yahoo bigotry, and his appallingly bad manners."

Conservative columnist William F. Buckley
Genuine Texas Handbook

☆ ☆ ☆

"Van Horn [Texas] is so healthy, we had to shoot a man to start a cemetery."

Bill Goynes, who coined this civic slogan for the town of Van Horn, then was gunned down during an argument and was the first man buried in the Van Horn cemetery in 1892
An Informal History of Texas

☆ ☆ ☆

"We must rebuild our communities one at a time."

Travis County District Attorney Ronnie Earle
Texas Monthly, November 1993

"Anybody leaves this rig, I'll beat the hell out of him."

Oil wildcatter, Houston politico, and natural-born leader of men Glenn McCarthy, to the crew on his first well
Genuine Texas Handbook

☆ ☆ ☆

"Your honor, the prosecutor is the only man I've ever met who can strut sitting down."

Defense attorney Temple Houston
An Informal History of Texas

☆ ☆ ☆

"You're not a real Texan till you've been kicked out of every decent state in America."

Joe Bob Briggs
Texas Is

23

24

"A born Texan has instilled in his system a mind-set of no retreat or no surrender. I wish everyone the world over had the dominating spirit that motivates Texans."

Former Texas Speaker of the House Billy Clayton
Texas Is

☆ ☆ ☆

"A certain amount of beer can make a man feel like he could beat cancer."

Author Larry L. King
Texas: A Self Portrait

"I've traveled all over the world, but I don't think there is any place better than Texas."

Oilwell firefighter Red Adair
Texas Is

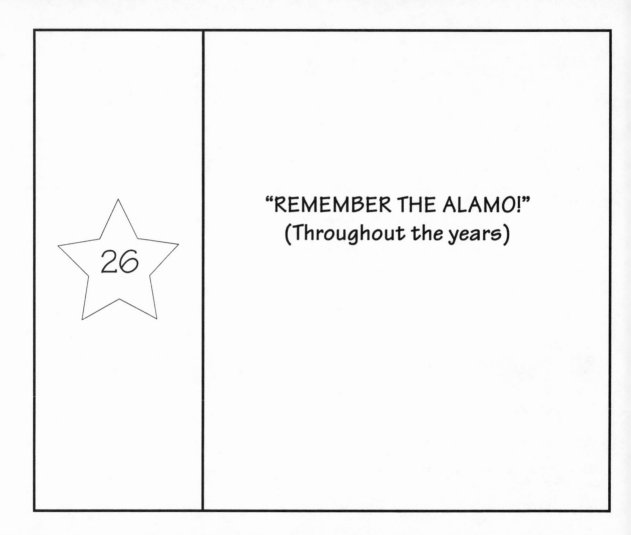

26

"REMEMBER THE ALAMO!"
(Throughout the years)

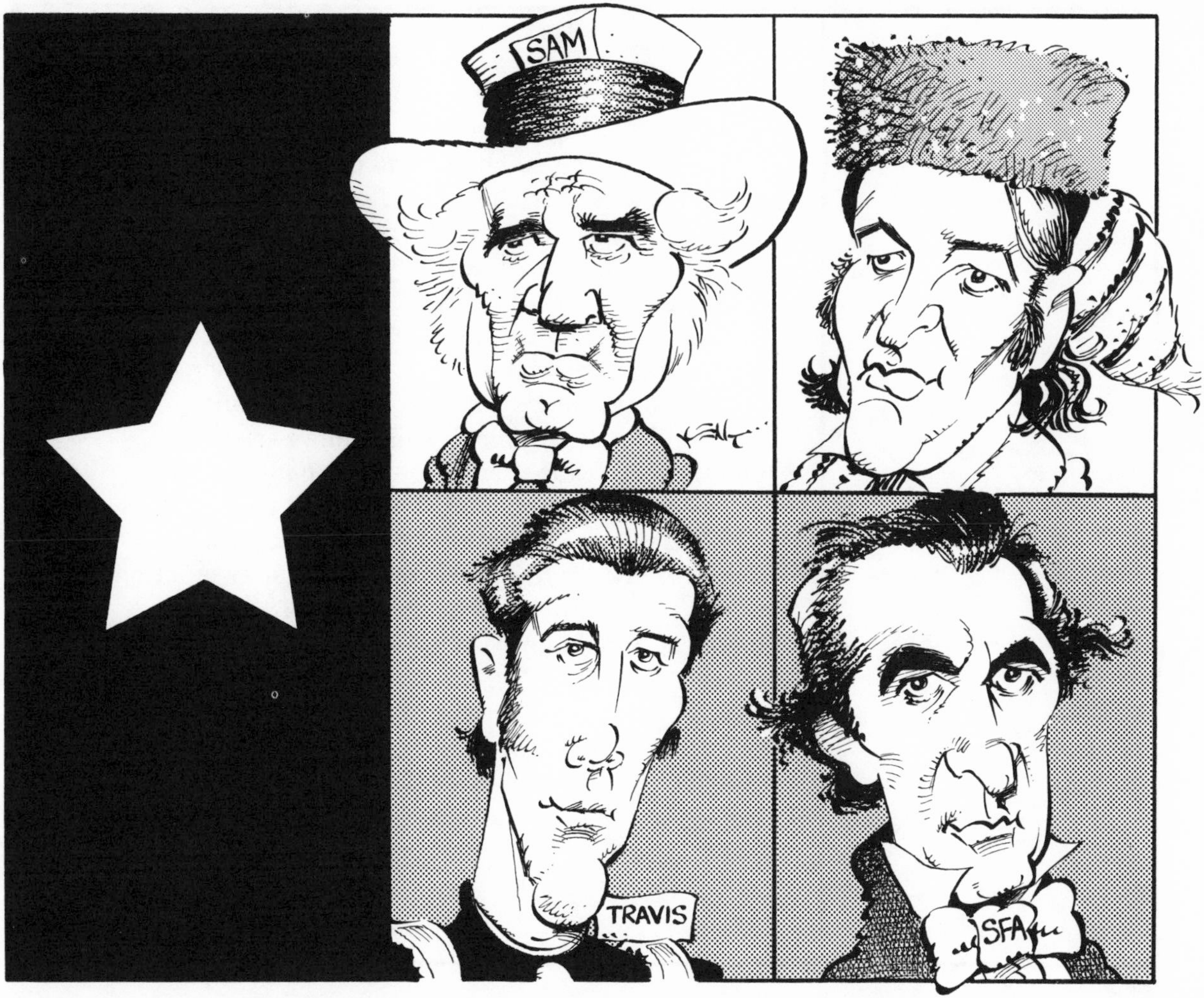
SAM
TRAVIS
SFA

A loose herd of Texas political writers and wranglers—ranging from Molly Ivins to Sam Attlesey to Sam Kinch, Jr. and others—have helped chronicle this ever-changing Texas political scene, which of course, is no different than it was 50 years ago or even 100 years ago.

Beginning with the days of Stephen F. Austin, famous Texas quotes have set our state apart from others throughout the years. Of course, the most famous is the Texas battle cry at San Jacinto, "Remember the Alamo!" This quote stirs the emotions of Texans today more than any other words, written or spoken. The second part of the battle cry, ". . . Remember Goliad!" has not persevered over the years, but was just as emotional to the Texans during that incredible 18-minute battle at San Jacinto.

☆ ☆ ☆

"Remember the Alamo! Remember Goliad!"

Battlecry of the Texans at the Battle of San Jacinto, 1836
Lone Star: A History of Texas and the Texans

"Indians in Texas are the readiest people with their weapons of all I have seen in the world."

Explorer Cabeza de Vaca, 1530
An Informal History of Texas

☆ ☆ ☆

"I am half horse, half alligator; a little touched with snapping turtle; can wade the Mississippi, leap the Ohio, ride upon a streak of lightening and slip without a scratch down a honey locust."

Davy Crockett, before he came to Texas
Texas Celebrates!

☆ ☆ ☆

"You go to hell. I'm going to Texas."

Davy Crockett, to the Tennessee Legislature, upon his defeat for re-election
Homesick Texan, Fall 1994

☆ ☆ ☆

"War is our only resource. We must defend our rights, ourselves and our country by force of arms."

Father of Texas Stephen F. Austin, 1835
Texas Celebrates!

30

"No frontiersman who has no other occupation than that of hunter will be received [in the new colony in Texas]. No drunkard, nor gambler, nor profane swearer; nor idler. . . ."

Stephen F. Austin, on his rules for his new Texas colony
Texas Monthly, November 1993

☆ ☆ ☆

"I shall never surrender or retreat. . . . If this call is neglected I am determined to sustain myself as long as possible and die like a soldier who never forgets what is due his honor and that of his country—VICTORY OR DEATH."

Colonel William Barrett Travis, excerpts from his 1836 letter from the Alamo
The Best of Texas

☆ ☆ ☆

"The Mexicans are upon us—give 'em hell!"

William Barrett Travis, 1836, giving his last order at the Battle of the Alamo
Lone Star: A History of Texas and the Texans

"Much of our success was due to Santa Anna's voluptuousness."

Private George Erath, on the Texans victory at San Jacinto, 1836
An Informal History of Texas

☆ ☆ ☆

"People who come to Texas these days are preachers, or fugitives from justice, or sons of bitches. Which one are you?"

Richard King, founder of the King Ranch
Texas Monthly, April 1994

☆ ☆ ☆

"Lawyers and doctors! It is not right that the people should be taxed for the education of such professional men, whose services are so extravagantly paid for."

Unattributed remark in Journal, Texas House of Representatives, 1858, during debate on establishment of a state university
Our Invaded Universities

31

"We are all vitally interested in defending and maintaining slavery. It cannot be destroyed without ruining and dishonoring every cotton state materially, morally, socially, and politically."

Editorial, *Texas State Gazette,* November 17, 1860, after Abraham Lincoln's election

☆ ☆ ☆

"He has all the characteristics of a dog except fidelity."

Then Governor of Texas Sam Houston on one of his political enemies, a secessionist leader, 1861
An Informal History of Texas

☆ ☆ ☆

"The hiss of the mob and howls of their jackal leaders cannot deter me nor compel me to take the oath of allegiance to a so-called Confederate Government."

Sam Houston, March, 1861
Secession and the Union in Texas

"If I owned Texas and Hell, I would rent out Texas and live in Hell."

General Philip H. Sheridan
An Informal History of Texas

☆ ☆ ☆

"The deceased came to his death at the hands of an unknown party who was a damn good pistol shot."

Judge Roy Bean
Texas Celebrates!

☆ ☆ ☆

"We have only two or three laws in Texas, such as against murder before witnesses and being caught stealing horses, and voting the Republican ticket."

Texas author O. Henry, circa 1890
The Establishment in Texas Politics

33

"Liberty is ever won by volunteers; the shackles of political and religious slavery are forged by the hands of hirelings. Prohibition cannot withstand the light of logic, the lessons of experience, nor the crucible, of the commonest kind of common sense."

Texas newspaper publisher William Brann
Iconoclast, 1897

☆ ☆ ☆

"We had to let a president of Humble [Ross Sterling] quit to become governor to establish proration."

Humble Oil Company executive, 1933
The Establishment in Texas Politics

☆ ☆ ☆

"The eyes of Texas are upon you."

Dr. William L. Prather, president of the University of Texas, to the school's students in 1903. Two students then wrote a song mocking Dr. Prather.
An Informal History of Texas

☆ ☆ ☆

"Damn this oil. I need water for my cows."

West Texas rancher and racing politico W. T. Waggoner, when he accidentally struck oil
Texas Celebrates!

34

"I will not deny that there are men in the district better qualified than I to go to Congress, but gentlemen, these men are not in the race."

Then Texas legislator Sam Rayburn, 1912, commenting on his election chances after personally drawing the boundaries of his district to eliminate any competition
The Years of Lyndon Johnson: The Path to Power

☆ ☆ ☆

"I'm in favor of doing anything we can to a Communist. We're going to crush them under our heels every way we can."

Governor Allan Shivers, 1954
Red Scare!

☆ ☆ ☆

"What Herman doesn't do."

Construction magnate George Brown, describing what he did in the construction firm Brown & Root, founded by his brother Herman Brown, circa 1928
The Years of Lyndon Johnson: The Path to Power

35

36

"The trouble with the nation's economy is simply Prohibition, which makes it possible for large-scale dealers in illicit liquor to amass tremendous amounts of currency; the present economic crisis is due to the withdrawal of billions of dollars from the channels of legitimate trade by these bootleggers."

Congressman Richard Kleberg, 1932
The Establishment in Texas Politics

☆ ☆ ☆

"We cannot put the ideology of Communism in an electric chair or in a prison. You cannot lynch Communism. You cannot burn Communism. If we, in fighting Communism, adopt totalitarian tactics, then we, by our own hands, will destroy ourselves."

Maury Maverick, Jr., 1954
Red Scare!

☆ ☆ ☆

"Carry only what money you need before you get to Texas. You will not be able to spend a dime in the state of Texas."

Postmaster General Jim Farley, 1933, advising congressmen leaving for a junket to Texas
The Years of Lyndon Johnson: The Path to Power

"Just as the time of Pericles was called the Golden Age of Athens so President Roosevelt's time will be called the Golden Age of Democracy."

Governor James V. Allred, 1937
The Establishment in Texas Politics

☆ ☆ ☆

"A congressman's first duty is to get re-elected."

Sam Rayburn, circa 1934
The Years of Lyndon Johnson: The Path to Power

☆ ☆ ☆

"In terms of extraordinary wealth, there is only one man—H. L. Hunt."

Envious multimillionaire J. Paul Getty
Genuine Texas Handbook

☆ ☆ ☆

"A Communist is a low creature with no respect for God, who does not believe in law, and is a cross between an anarchist and a fox."

Houston City Attorney Sewall Myer, 1939
Red Scare!

37

"I never like being called 'the most decorated' soldier. There were so many guys who should have gotten medals and never did—guys who were killed."

Texas-born World War II hero Audie Murphy
The Best of Texas

☆ ☆ ☆

"I find over here that most of the French and English believe that Texas is an independent nation now. I have talked with a lot of people who have heard of Texas, but who didn't know that it was supposed to be part of the U.S. I preach Texas day and night."

Major Homer Fry to Governor Beauford Jester, 1947, advocated Texas's secession from the Union.
The Establishment in Texas Politics

☆ ☆ ☆

"When we take up a fight, we've decided we're doing what is right for the people. From then on it's gloves off."

Martin Emmet Walters, editor
Houston Chronicle, 1948

38

"Christ's theory of brotherhood is the most radical theory ever created; and democracy is the most radical political idea man's ever had."

Robert Montgomery, University of Texas economic professor, 1948, explaining to a Texas legislature investigatory committee that he belonged to the two most radical organizations in existence, "the Methodist Church and the Democratic Party."
Our Invaded Universities

☆ ☆ ☆

"After that we had no trouble from the Communists around here. Everybody loves a winner. When the Commies were winning, they had support. Now we are in the saddle . . . that's the way it is, padnuh. People are sheep."

National Maritime Union anti-Communist crusader Tex George, 1948
Red Scare!

39

★ 40

"The Truman administration has left liberal democracy in the lurch. In this lurch, I and others turn to the Progressive Party headed by Henry Wallace. Mr. Truman's mediocrity of both mind and character leaves us no other alternative. He may mean well. Hell is paved with good intentions. Henry Wallace is in harmony with the inevitable evolution of society."

J. Frank Dobie, 1948
The Establishment in Texas Politics

☆ ☆ ☆

"Texas political leaders have plainly achieved the natural instinct for the low, disingenuous, fraudulent manipulations that constitute the art and mystery of politics under democracy."

Journalist and publisher H.L. Mencken, 1948
The Establishment in Texas Politics

☆ ☆ ☆

"I know keeping one's fellow man, no matter what color, down in ignorance is evil and undemocratic, and that such injustice results in evil to the oppressors as well as to the oppressed."

Professor J. Frank Dobie, during the Hemann Sweatt legal challenge for admission to the University of Texas School of Law, 1950
Red Scare!

"Why be stupid and weak when, with one drink, you can feel smart and strong?"

Sam Rayburn
Too Funny To Be President

☆ ☆ ☆

"Herman Brown is the most powerful man in Texas and close to bossing the entire state."

Houston political activist Hart Stilwell, 1951
The Establishment in Texas Politics

☆ ☆ ☆

"I am for Senator McCarthy because he is doing more than any other man to fight the Communist conspiracy in this country."

Houston millionaire and power broker Hugh Roy Cullen, 1954
Red Scare!

41

"When asked if he would introduce U.S. Senator Joe McCarthy to the state legislature, State Representative Maury Maverick Jr. said he would do it, but only if he could substitute Mickey Mouse for McCarthy. 'If we are going to get a rat to talk to us, at least let's get a good rat.'"

Author Richard Henderson
Maury Maverick: A Political Biography

☆ ☆ ☆

"These elements—the common national struggle, the unsettling effect of rapid change, the myths of Texanism—are in themselves almost enough to explain why Texas politics has taken on such a peculiar cast. But when all these elements are manipulated by clever men and by the kind of money the Little Rich—the prosperous car dealers, the contractors, the bottling concessionaires, the little oilmen, the real estate men—can make available to state candidate of their choice, these emotions can be made to stand up and march."

Historian Theodore H. White, 1954
The Establishment in Texas Politics

42

"The fact remains that any editor worth his salt knows that he is just about as dependent upon the public relations man as they are upon him. The task of covering the news has become a job of such magnitude and of such complexity that it cannot be done without help. No newspaper could afford the staff it would take to turn out the vast amount of news that fills the papers every day."

Journalist Stanley Kelley, Jr., 1956
The Establishment in Texas Politics

☆ ☆ ☆

"Who speaks for the Negro? Who speaks for him?"

Then State Senator Henry B. Gonzalez during a filibuster against Governor Price Daniels' segregation-preserving bills (1958)
Texas Celebrates!

☆ ☆ ☆

"Luckily for the free world, there were no 'Fifth Amendment' Texans at San Jacinto."

Senator Joseph McCarthy, April 21, 1954, at the San Jacinto Monument
Red Scare!

"Elkins doesn't practice law, he practices influence."

James V. Allred, describing Judge James A. Elkins, 1951
The Establishment in Texas Politics

☆ ☆ ☆

"Politics are not unlike war. Sometimes it is necessary to shoot from the hip."

Publisher Jesse Jones to Presidential candidate Dwight D. Eisenhower, 1952
Red Scare!

☆ ☆ ☆

"Any jackass can kick over a barn. It takes a carpenter to build one."

Sam Rayburn
Don't Throw Feathers at Chickens

☆ ☆ ☆

"It was part of the Texas ritual. We're rich as son-of-a-bitch stew but look how homely we are, just as folksy as Grandpappy back in 1836. We know about champagne and caviar but we talk hog and hominy."

Author Edna Ferber
Giant

44

"I tried to tell a joke once in a speech, and before I got through, I was the joke."

Sam Rayburn, 1960
The Years of Lyndon Johnson: The Path to Power

☆ ☆ ☆

"I want to say that I am not a slave and that I have the right to choose who my mate shall be without the dictation of any man. I have eyes and I have a heart, and when they fail to tell me who I shall have for mine I want to be put away in a lunatic asylum."

Jack Johnson, former heavyweight champion
The Best of Texas

☆ ☆ ☆

"I don't know anywhere else where the people of substance have this type of working political relationship to each other. You know, not like it's schemed out, but everybody just gets the idea and they go the same way."

Lawyer Ed Clark, 1960, while serving as a lobbyist in Texas
The Establishment in Texas Politics

45

46

"If our grandfathers had fought the Indians and the Redcoats like we are fighting the Communists, we wouldn't be alive today."

Unidentified concerned citizen quoted in William K. Kelley leaflet, 1961
The Establishment in Texas Politics

☆ ☆ ☆

"It's funny about Texans. They have to hate somebody, a whole lot of them."

Alla Clary, Sam Rayburn's secretary, 1969 (reminiscing about 1944)
The Establishment in Texas Politics

☆ ☆ ☆

"A Texan still can't go to New York yet without someone coming up and asking him to tell a funny story about Texas."

Texas historian A. C. Greene
Texas Celebrates!

"Republicans were in such short supply there was talk about establishing a reservation for them."

John Henry Faulk, recalling the days of a lopsided Democratic Texas
The Establishment in Texas Politics

47

48

"MY NAME IS TOWER,
BUT I DON'T."
(Politics in Washington, D.C.)

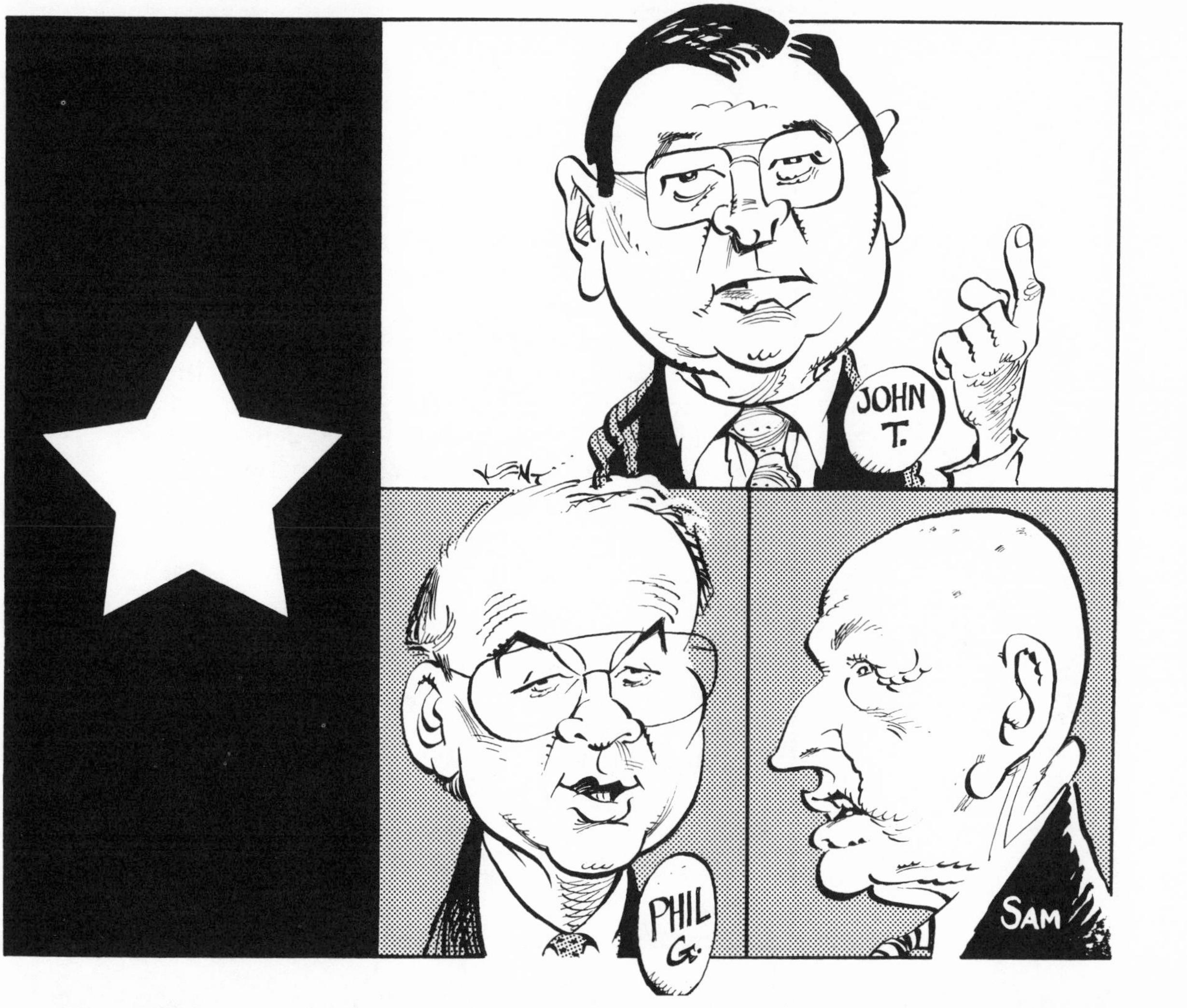
JOHN T.
PHIL G.
SAM

There is a club in Washington, D.C. for Texans in the nation's capital. The Texas State Society was founded in 1904, and it currently boasts 3,000 dues-paying members. In terms of size, prestige, tradition and fun, it is the envy of all organizations in Washington.

Texas has always had a large and powerful presence in Washington, especially during the tenures of House Speakers Sam Rayburn and Jim Wright, Presidents Lyndon Baines Johnson and George Bush, as well as diminutive Senator John Tower, who will always be remembered for his apt quote, "My name is Tower, but I don't."

☆ ☆ ☆

"Houston was adored by the people of Tennessee. And, as a favorite of Andrew Jackson's, it was confidently predicted that his next step in glory would be to the chair of the President of the United States."

Tennessee Governor Rufus Burleson on Sam Houston
An Informal History of Texas

50

"Texas is a state of mind. Texas is an obsession. Above all, Texas is a nation in every sense of the word."

Author John Steinbeck
The Best of Texas

☆ ☆ ☆

Democracy: "The system that substitutes election by the incompetent many for appointment by the corrupt few."

Playwright and political activist George Bernard Shaw
Don't Throw Feathers at Chickens

☆ ☆ ☆

"I'd feel a lot better if just one or two of them had ever run for sheriff."

U.S. Speaker of the House Sam Rayburn, on the youthful team that accompanied John F. Kennedy into the White House
Too Funny To Be President

51

"A hostile young man angrily accused U.S. House Speaker Sam Rayburn of being an old fogey. Rayburn replied. 'There's one thing worse than being an old fogey, and that's being a young fogey, Mr. Fogey.'"

Don't Throw Feathers at Chickens

☆ ☆ ☆

"You're going to hear a lot of laughing today. My doctor has given me orders that if I don't start laughing instead of cussing when I miss those shots, then he's going to stop me from playing golf. So every time I miss a shot today. I'm going to ho-ho-ho."

President Dwight D. Eisenhower
The Best of Texas

☆ ☆ ☆

"It's not worth a bucket of warm spit."

Vice President John Nance "Cactus Jack" Garner, on his assessment of the office
Don't Throw Feathers at Chickens

"I'm convinced that every boy, in his heart, would rather steal second base than an automobile."

U.S. Supreme Court Justice (and native Texan) Tom Clark
The Best of Texas

☆ ☆ ☆

"Look, if there's a hand grenade near our Dad, we want you on it first."

Jeb Bush to Republican strategist Lee Atwater, as the Bush brothers (Jeb and George W., Jr.) were questioning Atwater's loyalty to their father in the 1988 presidential campaign
D Magazine, April 1992

☆ ☆ ☆

"Joe McCarthy is a vigorous fellow, doing a fine job in a vigorous way."

Jesse Jones, 1952
Red Scare!

☆ ☆ ☆

"[Texas] is a reality check for the rest of the nation. Texans can see right through the bullshit people in other parts of the country might buy."

Molly Ivins
The Best of Texas

53

"All five of us are college graduates. My brother was the Army's first Hispanic four-star general. I'm the first Hispanic Cabinet Member. We were very fortunate. A certain amount of individual skill and commitment gets you a long way down the road."

Secretary of Education Lauro Cavazos, on his siblings and their upbringing as children of a King Ranch foreman
Texas Monthly, March 1989

☆ ☆ ☆

"A right is not what someone gives you; it's what no one can take away from you."

U.S. Attorney General (and native Texan) Ramsey Clark
The Best of Texas

☆ ☆ ☆

"I've read that Dan Quayle said the NAACP was out of touch, but that doesn't concern me very much, because if we're in touch with Dan Quayle, we're in trouble."

Gary Bledsoe
Texas Monthly, January 1992

54

"My best friends tend to be women. That's supposed to be characteristic of us Libras."

Senator John Tower
Texas Monthly, March 1989

☆ ☆ ☆

"Neither a wise man nor a brave man lies down on the tracks of history to wait for the train of the future to run over him."

Dwight D. Eisenhower
The Best of Texas

☆ ☆ ☆

"After 23 years of teaching economics in College Station and Washington, D.C., one thing is clear: Aggies are a lot smarter than congressmen."

Senator Phil Gramm
Texas Monthly, July 1990

55

"You've got the Speaker. You've got Sematech. You're going to have the next president. What are you going to do next? Move the Oregon national forest to Texas?"

Oregon Congressman Les AuCoin to Texas colleague Charles Wilson, on the Texas political-clout nationwide
Texas Monthly, March 1989

☆ ☆ ☆

"As Secretary of State, I am daily faced by challenges confronting the United States around the world. But I am also a public servant acutely aware of my duty to husband the taxpayer's dollars during a period of economic hardship here at home."

James A. Baker III
The Best of Texas

☆ ☆ ☆

"Read my lips: No new Texans."

Arizona Senator John McCain, at the Senate confirmation hearing of Secretary of Commerce Robert Mosbacher
Texas Monthly, March 1989

"I like power and I like to use it."

Sam Rayburn
The Best of Texas

☆ ☆ ☆

"The idea of just going out and making money for the sake of it doesn't interest me."

George Bush
Texas Monthly, March 1989

☆ ☆ ☆

"If [Ronald Reagan] had listened to me, he might still be broadcasting baseball today, probably in the big leagues, instead of traveling all over the country, as he did in 1976, looking for a job."

Singing cowboy (and native Texan) Gene Autry
The Best of Texas

☆ ☆ ☆

"We love your adherence to democratic principles."

George Bush, to Philippine President Ferdinand Marcos in 1981
Texas Monthly, March 1989

57

"I'd wear it in my navel for a million bucks."

Cosmetics executive Georgette Mosbacher, when asked if she was concerned about the curse of an Indian god for anyone wearing the Hope Diamond. She was wearing it to publicize a $1 million gift to the Smithsonian Institution, where it is usually on display.
Texas Monthly, January 1992

☆ ☆ ☆

"It's not what he doesn't know that bothers me; it's what he knows that just ain't so."

Will Rogers, on President Herbert Hoover
Don't Throw Feathers at Chickens

☆ ☆ ☆

"Of course it was good to see a Texan booted away from the Federal trough for once. You don't often get Texas's snout out of that sweet-smelling, ever-loving, money-packed trough. . . ."

Columnist Russell Baker, on Senator John Tower's being rejected for a Secretary of Defense nomination.
Texas Monthly, January 1990

58

"Jay Danforth Quayle III is a guy whose tongue is heavier than his brain."

Jim Hightower
Don't Throw Feathers at Chickens

☆ ☆ ☆

"Babbitt believes that the Iran-Contra hearings will establish conclusively that there is a link between Ronald Reagan and the Presidency."

Former Land Commissioner Bob Armstrong, on his friend, Arizona Governor and former Texan Bruce Babbitt.
Don't Throw Feathers at Chickens

☆ ☆ ☆

"Politics is played with a football, not a basketball. It takes real funny bounces."

Jack DeVore, longtime spokesperson for Lloyd Bentsen, to Sam Attlesey
Dallas Morning News

59

"I'm not so much concerned with the natural bastards as I am with the self-made ones."

U.S. Representative Bob Eckhardt, on Republicans who voted against funds for indigent children
Too Funny To Be President

☆ ☆ ☆

"When a drunk confronted Jim Wright in a Washington lounge, the stranger snarled. 'All Texas congressmen are rich, swaggering, uncouth braggarts.' Wright replied, 'Simply not true. We're not all rich.'"

Charles Herring, Jr., and Walter Richter
Don't Throw Feathers at Chickens

☆ ☆ ☆

"Stop working so hard."

U.S. Senator Kay Bailey Hutchison's mother's advice to her daughter
The Dallas Morning News, 1984

60

"Thank you for the compliment—but my family has lived north of the Rio Grande since 1710, and I imagine that's before your family left Ireland!"

U.S. Representative Kiki de la Garza, to a fellow U.S. Representative who complimented the Texan on his ability to speak English
Texas Is

☆ ☆ ☆

"Mrs. Robert Strauss answered her husband (former Democratic National Committee Chairman) when he wondered aloud how many truly wise men there were in the world. 'That's hard to tell,' she replied, 'but I imagine there's one less than you think there is.'"

Charles Herring, Jr., and Walter Richter
Don't Throw Feathers at Chickens

61

62

"To paraphrase that great Texan and patriot, Sam Houston, Texans have always known that a great destiny awaited them. This conviction has become part of the American tradition. We will always be indebted to Texas for its robust confidence in American values, and its pride in our contribution to western civilization."

General Alexander Haig
Texas Is

☆ ☆ ☆

"I'll bury my enemies face down, so that the harder they scratch to get out, the deeper they will go."

U.S. Senator Joe Bailey
Texas Celebrates!

"I'm reminded of a story told by Claude Pepper, the 87-year-old congressman from Florida. He said a stockbroker came up to him and said. 'This stock I'm offering you is certain to quadruple in three years.' Claude looked at him and replied, 'Son, at my age I don't even buy green bananas.'"

Texas Governor Ann Richards
Don't Throw Feathers at Chickens

64

"I AM FILLED WITH HUMIDITY."
(Politics in Austin)

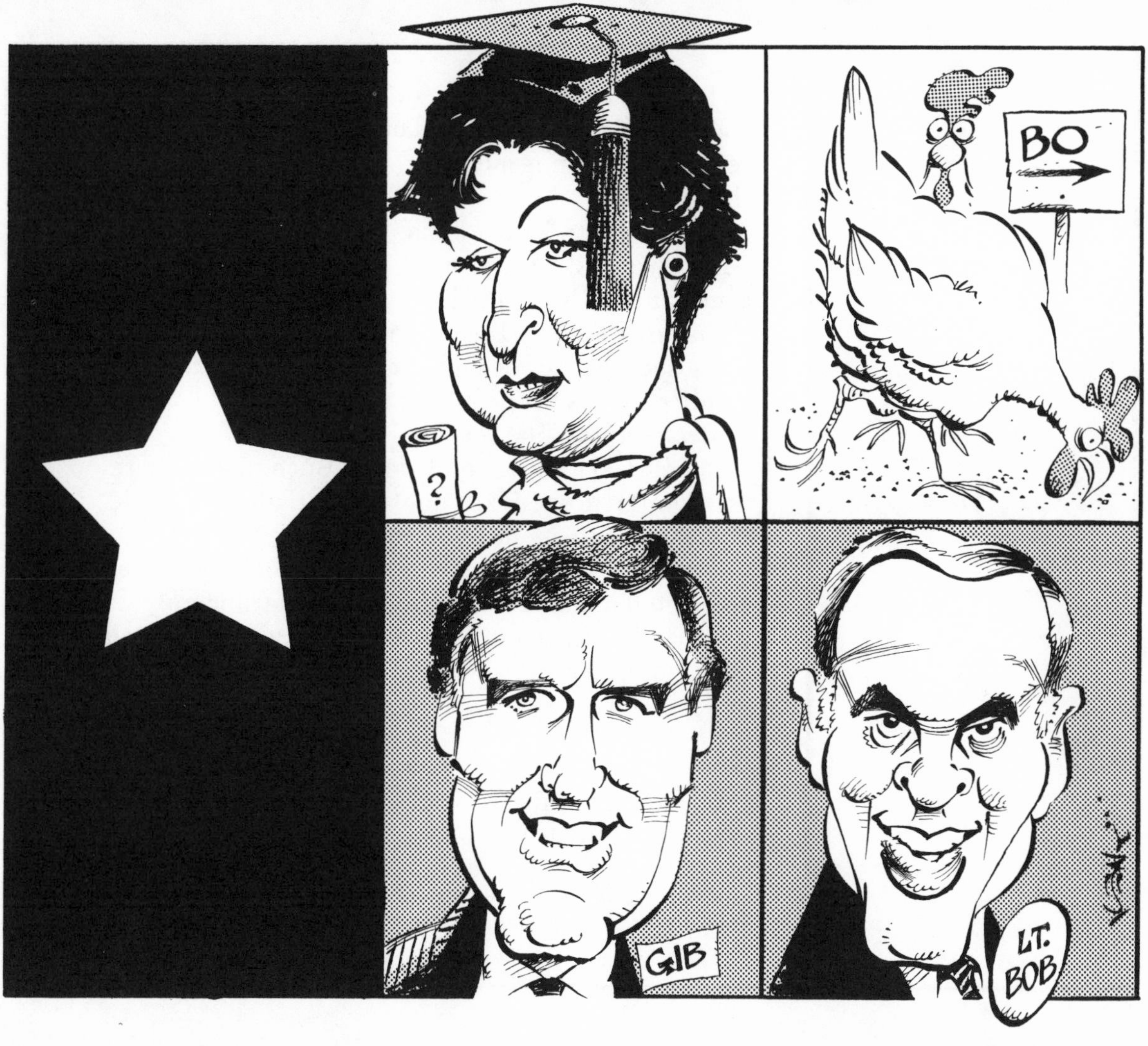

?
BO
GIB
LT. BOB

66

Texas is a unique place to begin with, but when you mix in our politics and our politicians, the final result in Austin is a bizarre stage unlike any other in the world.

The popular former Texas Speaker of the House Gib Lewis will be remembered forever for his unique command of the English language. Warning the House members of the potential bad results of a proposed bill, Lewis said, "It could have bad ramifistations in the hilterlands."

Between the likes of Jim Hightower, Lloyd Doggett, Carl Parker and Jerry Buchmeyer, there are enough great Texas quotes to fill another book. But the greatest one of all comes from the king of quotes, Gib Lewis, who was so overwhelmed at being re-elected as Speaker of the House, he sincerely admitted to the members of the House, "I am filled with humidity."

☆ ☆ ☆

"We should not fire people, but accomplish it through employee nutrition."

Texas Speaker of the House Gib Lewis on avoiding employee terminations while reducing the state's work force
Molly Ivins Can't Say That, Can She?

"Will all of you now please stand and be recognized?"

Gib Lewis, to a Texas House gallery packed with disabled citizens in wheelchairs
Don't Throw Feathers at Chickens

☆ ☆ ☆

"A teacher publicly challenged Gib Lewis' consistently bad syntax. 'What sin tax? I'm not for any sin tax. I'm against all new taxes.'"

Molly Ivins
The Texas Observer, February 14, 1992

☆ ☆ ☆

"Asking the Highway Department to accept changes to their policy to better protect the environment is like pulling teeth from a dinosaur."

Sierra Club leader Ken Kramer
Texas Weekly, March 25, 1991

☆ ☆ ☆

"It will improve the cumulative IQ of both parties."

State Democratic party executive director Ed Martin, on former gubernatorial candidate Andrew Briscoe's jump to the GOP
Texas Monthly, January 1988

67

68

"Now, I remember well my own commencement, and I think I can guess what you're feeling about right now."

Texas Railroad Commissioner Lena Guerrero, in a speech to Texas A&M graduates, *before* it was revealed she misrepresented that she had graduated from college.
Texas Monthly, November 1992

☆ ☆ ☆

"Perhaps you want something to be so much that you begin to believe it is."

Lena Guerrero, resigning as Railroad Commissioner, when it *was* revealed she had not graduated from college.
Texas Monthly, November 1992

☆ ☆ ☆

"What's the temperature in Railroad Commissioner Lena Guerrero's office? Minus one degree."

Austin American Statesman

"Do you realize that millions of Chinese are demonstrating for the right to carry on government the way we do?"

Representative Eddie Cavazos, while reviewing chaos on the House floor
Texas Weekly, June 5, 1989

☆ ☆ ☆

"I sat there during the first special session, fat, dumb and happy. I'm still fat, but I'm not as dumb and I'm not at all happy."

Representative Jim Parker, on sitting through multiple legislature sessions
Texas Weekly, December 4, 1989

☆ ☆ ☆

A former Dallas County commissioner tried to explain why he lost a re-election bid—illness and fatigue. In other words, he said, the voters were "sick and tired" of him.

Sam Attlesey
Dallas Morning News

69

"Everybody felt like they were watching their newborns go in for a tattoo."

Political consultant Monte Williams, describing the reaction of observers as the usual end of a session ensued
Texas Weekly, August 19, 1991

☆ ☆ ☆

"I did not hurt the citizens of the state at all by passing any legislation."

Representative John Cook, assessing his accomplishments after his first session
Texas Weekly, June 10,1991

☆ ☆ ☆

"After you've been in the House for 10 years, you ain't fit to be anything other than a senator."

Senator Carl Parker to Representative Gonzalo Barrientos when the latter moved from the House to the Senate
Texas Weekly, July 6, 1984

"I was very fortunate in my life to have some opportunities to do work which was particularly interesting. I might not have felt the same way if the work hadn't been so interesting, but for me it always was."

El Paso-born U.S. Supreme Court Justice Sandra Day O'Connor
The Best of Texas

☆ ☆ ☆

"I don't want to start any kind of precedent, but I do want to read your bill for a couple of minutes."

Senator Kent Caperton, prior to a vote on legislation (and referring to legislators voting on bills without reading them)
Texas Weekly, March 27, 1989

☆ ☆ ☆

"Young man, when you are 86 years old, you don't give a damn who your state senator is!"

A little old lady, through a locked screen door, when Bill Sarpalius requested her support as he was going door-to-door campaigning for the Texas Senate
Don't Throw Feathers at Chickens

71

72

"I'm not necessarily saying the man's gay, I'm just saying he's wimpish. I think he's like a man who could possibly wear lace on his underwear."

Fringe candidate W. N. Otwell on Democratic gubernatorial candidate Jim Mattox
Texas Weekly, October 9, 1989

☆ ☆ ☆

"Jim Mattox has brought disgrace, fiscal irresponsibility and scandal to the office [of Attorney General]."

Opponent Roy Barrera, Jr., who added that he was not going to engage in mudslinging
Molly Ivins Can't Say That, Can She?

☆ ☆ ☆

"There ain't nothing in the middle of the road but yellow stripes and dead armadillos."

Jim Hightower, on political neutrality
Texas Weekly, July 23, 1984

"The people have a right to know how elected officials make—or, in my case, lose—their money."

Land Commissioner Garry Mauro
Texas Weekly, April 15, 1991

☆ ☆ ☆

"I was going on and on about my friend George Shipley, and how wonderful he was. Finally, my new friend [a newly-elected state representative colleague] asked me who was this guy George Shipley. 'He's a well-known pollster,' I replied. 'Oh, yeah,' said the new representative quite seriously, 'What does he upholster?'"

State Representative Steve Wolens
Don't Throw Feathers at Chickens

☆ ☆ ☆

"Letting the fox in the hen house to guard the chickens generally results in larger foxes and fewer eggs."

Political journalist Sam Kinch, Jr., quoted from an anti-branch banking election brochure
Texas Weekly, October 6, 1986

73

74

"The press is like a bunch of chiggers—they won't eat you but they'll bite you where it's embarrassing to scratch."

Former State Bar President Joe Nagy
Texas Weekly, June 27, 1988

☆ ☆ ☆

"The keen scatological interest of most reporters originally prompted me to schedule the operation in the Capitol press room. My doctors, however, advised me to seek more sanitary conditions."

Bob Bullock, after observing a little too much glee over his hemorrhoid surgery
Don't Throw Feathers at Chickens

☆ ☆ ☆

"[My new job as Lieutenant Governor-Elect was] kind of like being an unemployed king."

Comptroller Bob Bullock, after the 1990 election
Texas Weekly, January 28, 1991

"It's a marvelous piece of paper. It improves your personality. Your jokes are funnier when you have one of those things."

Lieutenant Governor Bill Hobby, on a formal election certificate
Texas Weekly, December 17, 1990

☆ ☆ ☆

"Politicians are like a bunch of bananas. They are pretty yellow, they are all a little crooked and they hang together."

A lobbyist, overheard in the Texas Senate lounge
Don't Throw Feathers at Chickens

☆ ☆ ☆

"I wouldn't want to say Bullock was boring, but it was the only time Senator Parker and I ever slept together."

State Senator Cyndi Taylor Krier, referring to the effect of a long speech by Bob Bullock to the Texas Senate, where Krier had been feuding for some time with Carl Parker
Don't Throw Feathers at Chickens

75

"Bob Bullock doesn't have a lot of friends. He does have a lot of ex-wives. He's the only person I know whose marriage license reads, 'To whom it may concern.'"

Lieutenant Governor Bill Hobby
Don't Throw Feathers at Chickens

☆ ☆ ☆

"Ten kids in 13 years. The woman had to run for the state legislature just to get out of the house."

Ann Richards, on Representative Nancy McDonald mothering 10 children in 13 years, at a Mental Health Association Roast

☆ ☆ ☆

"I get along well with women. I've been married five times—and they are supporting me 3 to 2."

Bob Bullock
Don't Throw Feathers at Chickens

☆ ☆ ☆

"[Gib Lewis] is so unethical, he probably shoots quail on the ground."

Political opponent Charles Gore
Texas Weekly, August 6, 1990

"Kinda like people slowing down at a wreck on a highway to see the dead."

Republican political consultant Rob Allyn, on America's fascination with Texas Politics
Texas Weekly, December 3, 1990

☆ ☆ ☆

"How many federal judges does it take to change a lightbulb? Only one. He just holds onto the bulb— and the universe revolves around him."

Jerry Buchmeyer
Texas Lawyer, January 29, 1990

☆ ☆ ☆

"Chief Justice John Marshall once said to make a good judge you had to have the ability 'to look a lawyer straight in the face for two solid hours and not hear a damn word he says.'"

Jerry Buchmeyer
Texas Lawyer, January 29, 1990

77

78

"In political combat, as in speed contests among horses, the outcome becomes doubtful only after the entry of the second contestant."

West Texas trial lawyer Warren Burnett
"Observations on the Direct Election Method of Judicial Selection," 44 Tex. L. Rev. 1098, 1099 (1966)

☆ ☆ ☆

"How can you be a good judge? I've learned you've got to do it every day. One day of being a good judge is like one day of clean living. It just ain't gonna help."

Jerry Buchmeyer
Texas Lawyer, January 29, 1990

☆ ☆ ☆

"I have mixed emotions about Bob Bullock. Mixed emotions are when your daughter comes home from the prom with a Gideon Bible."

Jim Hightower
Don't Throw Feathers at Chickens

"I just can't look at Jim Hightower without thinking about pig droppings."

Bob Bullock
Don't Throw Feathers at Chickens

☆ ☆ ☆

"Being a good judge is not that hard. The secret is to act as if you've known all of your life what you just learned five minutes ago."

Jerry Buchmeyer
Texas Lawyer, January 29, 1990

☆ ☆ ☆

"This is a whole lot like when the Legislature is in session. The only difference is that today we have adult supervision."

Representative Fred Hill, observing a kiddie Easter-egg hunt in the House chamber
Don't Throw Feathers at Chickens

☆ ☆ ☆

"The folks you help won't remember it and the folks you hurt won't ever forget it."

Bill Clayton
Texas Weekly, June 25, 1984

79

"I am like the mouse that just got caught. I don't want more cheese. I just want out of the trap."

Representative Sam Russell on controversial votes, which inevitably offend one constituent group or another.
Texas Weekly, March 16, 1987

☆ ☆ ☆

"Statistics are very difficult for me because I can't add or multiply. Somewhere in my life I lost the ability to do that; that's why I am a lawyer."

Representative Mike Martin
Don't Throw Feathers at Chickens

☆ ☆ ☆

"Any time two friends agree on everything, one of them is unnecessary."

Bob Bullock
Don't Throw Feathers at Chickens

☆ ☆ ☆

"Mr. Speaker, I raise a point of order that this is a battle of wits and both parties are unarmed."

Representative Herman Jones, on an argument between "two of our less brilliant" state representatives
Don't Throw Feathers at Chickens

"Listen, Mr. Hutchison, I can explain the bill for you *but I can't understand it for you!*"

Then Representative Carl Parker to Representative Ray Hutchison, after Hutchison kept asking the same question over and over concerning Parker's proposed bill
Don't Throw Feathers at Chickens

☆ ☆ ☆

"Yes, you may speak briefly on this issue, but I doubt that you can."

Bill Hobby to Senator Babe Schwartz, the long-winded state senator who requested to speak briefly on an issue
Don't Throw Feathers at Chickens

☆ ☆ ☆

"For the first time in history, BS is going to flow from the countryside to the state capitol."

Jim Hightower, on learning that the City of Austin was buying electrical power generated from West Texas feedlot residue
Don't Throw Feathers at Chickens

81

"If I ever find one woman willing to marry an Aggie politician, I don't want to give her a chance to change her mind."

Senator Chet Edwards, on his opposition to a pending Senate bill creating a delay between the purchase of a marriage license and the marriage
Don't Throw Feathers at Chickens

☆ ☆ ☆

"Proposing taxes at any time is kind of like milking an alligator—fraught with danger from both ends."

Senator Chet Brooks
Texas Weekly, September 1, 1986

☆ ☆ ☆

"It is going to be like drinking picante sauce straight out of the bottle."

Representative Stan Schlueter, on a particularly stout tax bill
Texas Weekly, October 6, 1986

☆ ☆ ☆

"Everyone wants to cut spending, but not in their own districts. It's kind of like everyone wants to go to heaven but no one wants to die to get there."

Texas Comptroller John Sharp
The Dallas Morning News, March 6, 1992

"It's kind of like drinking out of a spittoon—if you've got to do it, do it in one gulp."

Representative David Counts, reacting to proposals for deep budget cuts, resulting from a series of rigorous agency audits
Texas Weekly, July 1, 1991

☆ ☆ ☆

"Senator, you married into all your money, but every dime I have was earned right here on the floor of the Senate."

Senator Bill Moore, comparing his source of income to another senator's
Don't Throw Feathers at Chickens

☆ ☆ ☆

"Gib Lewis' defense to a charge of having omitted an oil well, an airplane and a company from a financial disclosure statement: 'I ran out of room on the paper.'"

Molly Ivins
Molly Ivins Can't Say That, Can She?

83

84

"If you rob Peter to pay Paul, you can always count on the support of Paul."

Representative Ted Kamel
Texas Weekly, September 23, 1991

☆ ☆ ☆

"What we need is a one-armed federal judge who can't say, 'on the other hand . . .'."

Representative Mark Stiles
Texas Weekly, August 5, 1991

☆ ☆ ☆

"Texas politicians aren't crooks: it's just that they tend to have an overdeveloped sense of extenuatin' circumstance. As they say around the Legislature, if you can't drink their whiskey, screw their women, take their money, and vote against 'em anyway, you don't belong in office."

Molly Ivins, on the traditional legislator-lobbyist relationship
Molly Ivins Can't Say That, Can She?

"I am a retired sinner, but I do come out of retirement now and then."

Senator V. E. "Red" Berry
Don't Throw Feathers at Chickens

☆ ☆ ☆

"He's a lot like the weather in West Texas—thunders a lot but never rains."

Senator Bill Sims, on a colleague's struggle with ethics reforms
Texas Weekly, June 11, 1987

☆ ☆ ☆

"I keep telling myself, 'Remember, you've got an indoor job. It beats picking cotton.'"

John Hall, Chairman of the Texas Natural Resource Conservation Commission
Texas Monthly, September 1994

☆ ☆ ☆

"As with [Lyndon] Johnson, what I remember most about [Bill] Clements is the ferocity of character."

Texas Observer publisher Ronnie Dugger
Texas Celebrates!

85

86

"If God Almighty Hisself wanted to try to create Earth today, he couldn't get a permit to do it."

Bob Leach, on the Legislature's overregulation
Texas Weekly, May 18, 1987

☆ ☆ ☆

"Everybody is looking at the price-tag of this bill. What we really need is a fiscal impact statement on the cost of ignorance."

Carl Parker, on the opposition of a school-finance reform bill
Texas Weekly, March 26, 1990

☆ ☆ ☆

"God bless Texas."

Bob Bullock, on how he closes every public appearance
Texas Monthly, September 1994

"Cooperation has been explained to me in Austin as an unnatural act between non-consenting adults."

Candidate for Lieutenant Governor Rob Mosbacher on the popularity of political fisticuffs
Texas Weekly, April 16, 1990

☆ ☆ ☆

"I have always been a large contributor to politics."

Bo Pilgrim, after handing out blank $10,000 checks on the floor of the Texas Senate
Texas Monthly, September 1994

87

88

"I've never had splinters in my crotch from straddling fences on issues."

Personal Communication Representative Robert Turner, 1994

☆ ☆ ☆

"He always did want to be the Speaker."

Molly Ivins, on Representative Mike Martin of Longview, who hired his cousin to shoot him in the arm, then claimed he was the victim of a satanic and Communistic cult retaliating against his pro-family and pro-American positions. When the law uncovered his scheme, he hid out at his mother's house, where he was found in a stereo cabinet.
Molly Ivins Can't Say That, Can She?

"We're not criminalizing the buying of football players. We're just regulating the price."

Carl Parker, on proposed legislation creating penalties for illegal payments to college players
Texas Weekly, March 13, 1989

☆ ☆ ☆

"What better place to start in our fight against ignorance than right here in Austin when the Legislature is in session?"

Texas Education Commissioner W. N. Kirby to Sam Attlesey
The Dallas Morning News

89

90

"JUST RELAX AND ENJOY IT."
(The Governorship)

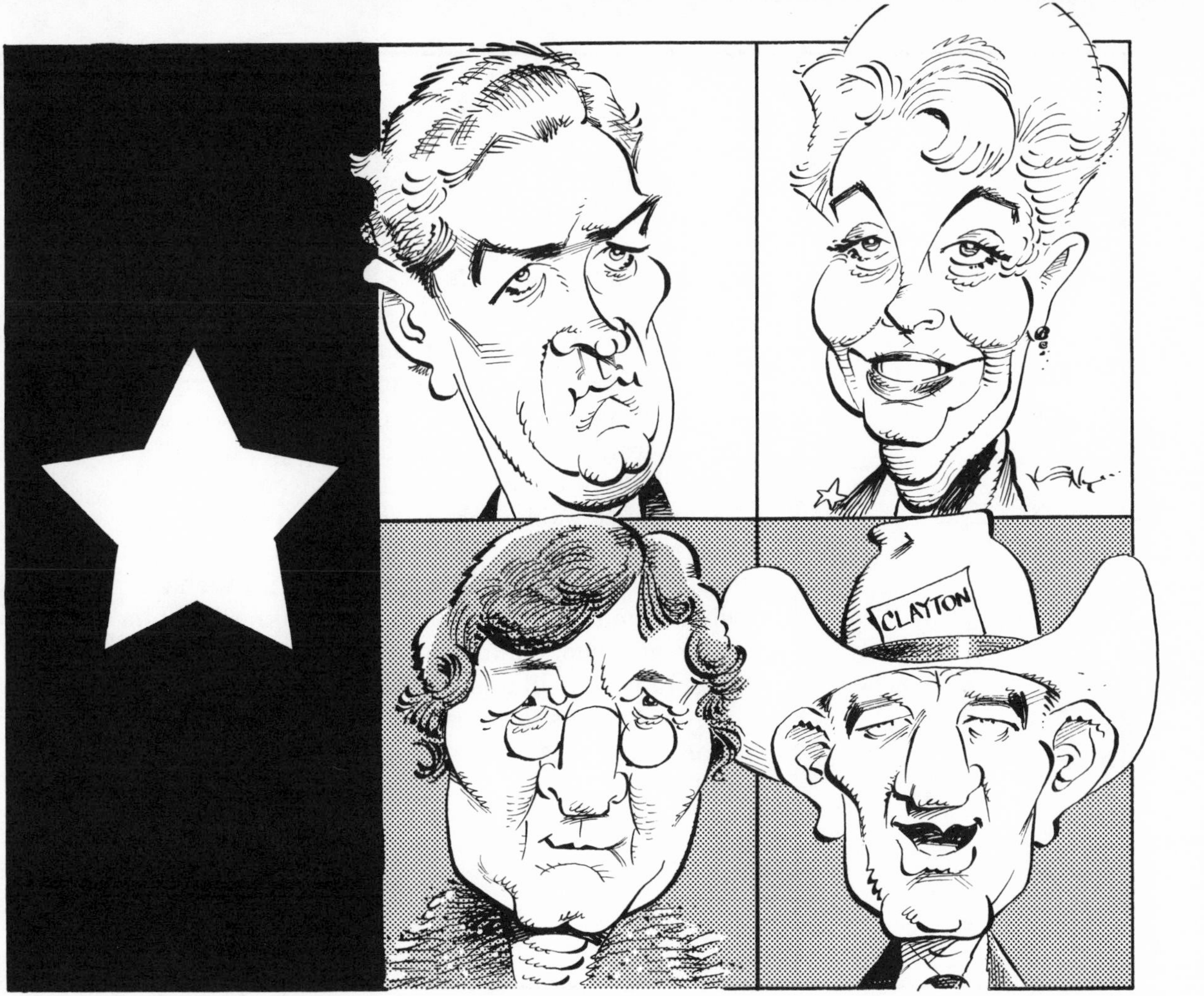
CLAYTON

The spirit of the Texas political world begins and ends with the governor.

Although the governor of Texas has little real power, the image of the office has always cast a long shadow over the Lone Star State. From the early days of Sam Houston to today's current resident of the governor's mansion, many of the governors' quotes have reflected the unique Texas state of mind.

It is ironic that the most famous quote of all actually kept the man who said it from becoming governor. Republican gubernatorial candidate Clayton Williams of Midland enjoyed a commanding lead over his Democratic opponent Ann Richards when a bad case of "boot-in-mouth" knocked him out of the governor's mansion. The quote which will live in infamy is Williams' line to a group of reporters out on his ranch as the weather started to turn nasty: "Bad weather is like rape. If it's inevitable, just relax and enjoy it."

"I have found far more disloyalty in the state university at Austin than among the Germans or the people of any other nationality."

Governor James E. "Pa" Ferguson, 1917
Our Invaded Universities

☆ ☆ ☆

"I'm for the *home.* If that be treason, make the most of it."

James "Pa" Ferguson, circa 1920
The Establishment in Texas Politics

☆ ☆ ☆

"Two Governors for the price of one."

Miriam A. "Ma" Ferguson, campaigning for Governor in 1924 after husband James "Pa" Ferguson had been impeached, convicted, and removed from the office.
The Establishment in Texas Politics

93

"Should Spanish-speaking children be punished for speaking Spanish in Texas schools? If the English language was good enough for Jesus Christ, it is good enough for the children of Texas."

Miriam A. "Ma" Ferguson
Don't Throw Feathers at Chickens

☆ ☆ ☆

"Texas could exist without the United States, but the United States cannot, except at very great hazard, exist without Texas."

Sam Houston
The Best of Texas

☆ ☆ ☆

"Margaret. Texas."

Sam Houston's dying words, July 26, 1863
An Informal History of Texas

94

"When Jim 'Pa' Ferguson was on the gubernatorial campaign trail, he got a phone call from his campaign manager in Dallas. 'Jim, you better get yourself up here to Dallas in a hurry. Your opposition is telling the durn'est pack of lies on you that you can imagine.' Ferguson replied. 'Dallas, hell! I gotta get to Houston. I got much worse problems down there. My enemies are all over town down there and they're telling the truth on me!'"

Former State Senator Tom Creighton, on "Pa" Ferguson's campaigning
Don't Throw Feathers at Chickens

☆ ☆ ☆

"The President [of the United States] is of the opinion that your right to the office of governor at this time is at least so doubtful that he does not feel warranted in furnishing U.S. Troops."

President Ulysses S. Grant, to Texas Governor E. J. Davis, who had been defeated for re-election by Richard Coke, but had taken up arms to stay in office, 1873
An Informal History of Texas

"My father resigned as governor of one state because of the love of a woman, and he resigned as the governor of another state because of his love for his country."

Temple Houston
An Informal History of Texas

☆ ☆ ☆

"When Texas united her destiny with that of the United States, she entered not into the North or South; her connection was not sectional, but national."

Sam Houston
The Best of Texas

☆ ☆ ☆

"Now, you'll have to talk to Jim about that. His office is downstairs."

Miriam A. "Ma" Ferguson to a gentleman who accidentally bumped into her on the second floor of the Capitol and said "Oh, pardon me, Governor."
Don't Throw Feathers at Chickens

96

"Less Johnson grass and politicians, more smokestacks and businessmen."

Campaign slogan, William Lee "Pappy" O'Daniel, 1938, running for Texas governor
The Establishment in Texas Politics

☆ ☆ ☆

"Had William Lee 'Pappy' O'Daniel been even slightly less astute, had he made a slightly less careful analysis of his own talents and the emotional requirements of his constituents, he might very well have gone on the road with a medicine show."

George Sessions Perry, 1942
Red Scare!

☆ ☆ ☆

"When you're out of office, you can be a statesman."

Former Governor John Connally
The Best of Texas

97

"It's a good thing John Connally wasn't at the Alamo. He'd be organizing Texans for Santa Anna."

Liz Carpenter, when party-switching former Governor John Connally said he'd head Richard Nixon's 1972 campaign
Don't Throw Feathers at Chickens

☆ ☆ ☆

"I feel like a piece of bread between two slices of ham."

John Connally, on being seated between humorists Cactus Pryor and Morris Frank, both of whom had worked the governor over at a Houston banquet.
Inside Texas

☆ ☆ ☆

"Anyone who owns agricultural land should have the right to drill their own wells. To do otherwise would go against our founding fathers."

Mrs. Dolph Briscoe, on why voters in Uvalde and Medina counties rejected a regional water-conservation plan.
Texas Monthly, January 1990

98

"[Dolph Briscoe has] all the charisma of bread pudding."

Molly Ivins
Texas Monthly, November 1992

☆ ☆ ☆

"Turkey feathers and deer tracks make mighty thin soup."

Then State Treasurer Ann Richards, describing the lean diet resulting from the tax short fall
Texas Weekly, June 18, 1984

☆ ☆ ☆

"The man's peerless imitation of a weather vane has helped spread the impression that he can't go to the bathroom without consulting the polls."

Molly Ivins on Governor Mark White
Molly Ivins Can't Say That, Can She?

☆ ☆ ☆

"I'm not surprised. If the state had a boat he'd sell that, too. He thinks the world is flat."

Bob Bullock, on Governor William P (Bill) Clements, Jr.'s budget-cutting, including elimination of a state airplane
Don't Throw Feathers at Chickens

99

100

"Oh, good. Now he'll be bi-ignorant."

Jim Hightower, on Gov. Bill Clements studying Spanish
Molly Ivins Can't Say That, Can She?

☆ ☆ ☆

"Bill Clements was a self-made man before the days of quality control."

Garry Mauro
Don't Throw Feathers at Chickens

☆ ☆ ☆

"He's a man of his most recent word."

Lloyd Doggett, on Bill Clements
D Magazine, January 1988

☆ ☆ ☆

"And I hope that gap gets wider."

Bill Clements, who opposed a pay raise for legislators, after someone pointed out the substantial disparity between the governor's $91,600 salary and the $340 a month that those legislators were taking home
Don't Throw Feathers at Chickens

"I don't have to go through a trial and error period with (the legislature). It's like two old dogs smelling each other."

Bill Clements
D Magazine, January 1988

☆ ☆ ☆

"We have extracted a thorn in the side of everyone concerned from the Agriculture Commissioner [Jim Hightower] and we have put it in the hands of experts."

Bill Clements, after his successful bid to remove pesticide regulation from Jim Hightower
D Magazine, January 1990

☆ ☆ ☆

"As I have traveled around this state, many people have said to me, 'Texas will never be Texas again.' But I say they are wrong. I say Texas will always be Texas."

Representative Tom Loeffler
Molly Ivins Can't Say That, Can She?

"I plan to stand up and be counted. And the thing I'm gonna do is, I'm gonna do what we're gonna do right now. I'm going to the people and say, 'Now this is what I'm trying to do.' And I'm going to do this because I believe the people need representation."

Gubernatorial candidate Paul Eggers
Molly Ivins Can't Say That, Can She?

☆ ☆ ☆

"I like the Christmas star. Maybe it will attract some wise men."

Ann Richards, when asked by a reporter what should be on top of the Capitol during the restoration of the Goddess of Liberty
Don't Throw Feathers at Chickens

☆ ☆ ☆

"Here is my Ten Point Plan to Improve Texas Education."

Jack Rains, 1990 Republican gubernatorial candidate, who was then reminded by the press that his plan had only nine points
Don't Throw Feathers at Chickens

102

"Vote for Jim Mattox. He hasn't been endorsed by anyone on death row."

1990 Texas Democratic Primary gubernatorial candidate Jim Mattox, after finding a prison newsletter that endorsed Ann Richards
Molly Ivins Can't Say That, Can She?

☆ ☆ ☆

"I feel very fortunate, truthfully, that there was a treatment program for my disease [alcoholism]. I wish there were a treatment program for meanness, and then maybe Jim Mattox could get well."

Ann Richards
Texas Weekly, March 12, 1990

☆ ☆ ☆

"Ginger Rogers did everything Fred Astair did. She just did it backwards and in high heels."

Ann Richards

☆ ☆ ☆

"I learned more from failure than any success."

Ann Richards
The Best of Texas

103

"You know what AA [Alcoholics Anonymous] is for? It's not to tell you to stop drinking. It's to remind you of who you were."

Ann Richards
Texas Monthly, April 1994

☆ ☆ ☆

"Ann Richards would save the state $5,000 a year if she'd give up Spray Net."

Cactus Pryor
Don't Throw Feathers at Chickens

☆ ☆ ☆

"I've always said that in politics, your enemies can't hurt you, but your friends will kill you."

Ann Richards
Texas Monthly, April 1994

☆ ☆ ☆

"Ann Richards can't help it. She was born with silver roots in her hair."

Kay Bailey Hutchison
D Magazine, January 1993

"Let me tell you, sisters, seeing dried egg on a plate in the morning is a lot dirtier than anything I've had to deal with in politics."

Ann Richards
Texas Monthly, October 1990

☆ ☆ ☆

"Ann Richards is a political ambulance-chaser. Asking Ann Richards to solve the insurance problem is like asking the Boston Strangler for a neck massage."

Gordon Hensley, Clayton Williams' spokesman
Texas Weekly, December 22, 1990

☆ ☆ ☆

"When the thought of politics came up, wanting to be governor of Texas someday was the first and only thing that came to mind. It's natural for anybody growing up in the state to think about it. For most of my life, it was the only political idea I ever had."

Former Texas Ranger and Houston Astro pitcher Nolan Ryan
Ultra, March 1990

105

"He's a good man, he's got a good business mind, he will do a good job, he's my kind of guy, and he's my second cousin."

Oilfield services magnate Eddie Chiles, on why he supported gubernatorial candidate Clayton Williams
Texas Weekly, July 31, 1989

☆ ☆ ☆

"When our kids get on drugs, that's when Clayton Williams is going to introduce them to the joys of bustin' rocks."

Gubernatorial candidate Clayton Williams
Texas Monthly, October 1990

☆ ☆ ☆

"It was a lot different in those days. The houses were the only place you got serviced then."

Clayton Williams, elaborating on his visiting brothels in Mexico as a teenager.
Texas Monthly, October 1990

"Claytie was just a normal, red-blooded boy who loved to have a good time and occasionally got into trouble feeling his oats."

Chicora Williams, mother of Clayton Williams
Texas Monthly, October 1990

☆ ☆ ☆

"I'm not going to force anybody to wear cowboy hats, jeans, and act like I do. But I've noticed that most people who hang around me long enough wind up owning a pair of boots."

Clayton Williams
Texas Monthly, October 1990

☆ ☆ ☆

"Bad weather is like rape. If it's inevitable, just relax and enjoy it."

Clayton Williams
Texas Monthly, October 1990

107

"When oil was $40 a barrel, I used to be six-foot-four. Now I'm four-foot-six, but I'm still here."

Clayton Williams
Texas Monthly, October 1990

☆ ☆ ☆

"People may not like what Claytie says, but they admire him for his candor."

Buddy Barfield, Clayton Williams campaign manger, after some of Williams' controversial statements
Texas Monthly, October 1990

☆ ☆ ☆

"Tom Luce got kinda stern with me during one of the debates. He questioned whether Texas can ride horseback into the twenty-first century. Well, my answer to that is that you can if you have a good horse."

Clayton Williams
Texas Monthly, October 1990

"When the owner of the Astros and the owner of the Rangers are in Pittsburgh for a meeting, who do you think gets interviewed?"

Dallas sports personality Norm Hitzges, on George W. Bush's star power as a part owner of the Rangers
D Magazine, April 1992

☆ ☆ ☆

"Back when dinosaurs roamed the earth and I was your age, politics was a male province. Women made the coffee, and men made the decisions."

Ann Richards, to the 1992 graduating class of Smith College
Texas Monthly, July 1992

☆ ☆ ☆

"I want the folks to see me sitting in the same seat they sit in, eating the same popcorn, peeing in the same urinal."

George W. Bush, on sitting in the stands (behind the dugout) instead of a private suite at the baseball park in Arlington
Time Magazine, 1992

109

"Nellie and I worked hard all of our lives to make sure our future would be financially secure. Well, the future is here, and things haven't quite worked out like we'd planned. But that's all right because there's no better place than Texas to start over and to save a little."

John Connally, after filing for bankruptcy
Texas Monthly, January 1989

☆ ☆ ☆

"He attended Greenwich Country Day and I went to San Jacinto High School in Midland, Texas."

George W. Bush when asked how he is different from his dad
D Magazine, April 1992

☆ ☆ ☆

"You know, there are a lot of would-be governors of Texas sitting around today who never took the opportunity to get into a race when the time was right. If George is good at anything, it's timing."

Laura Bush, wife of George W. Bush
Texas Monthly, May 1994

110

"The reason people can relate to baseball is that it's the sport that normal-sized people can play."

George W. Bush
D Magazine, April 1992

☆ ☆ ☆

"I know that you would have liked to have the most famous Bush here tonight, but my mother was busy."

George W. Bush's frequent opening line while campaigning for governor

☆ ☆ ☆

"Don't underestimate this guy. He's no doubt the biggest political animal in the family—and clearly more competitive than his father."

Fred McClure, former senior legislative aide to President Bush, on George W. Bush
Texas Monthly, May 1994

☆ ☆ ☆

"While the proceeds of the lottery are not large enough to solve all of our school funding needs, they should be dedicated solely to education."

George W. Bush
The Dallas Morning News, October 16, 1994

111

"When lottery ticket sales are down, education suffers. It's not a good idea to tie education to something so unpredictable."

Ann Richards
The Dallas Morning News, October 16, 1994

☆ ☆ ☆

"They'll like me too, if they just get a whiff of me."

George W. Bush, on the Texas GOP voters he met during the gubernatorial campaign
Texas Monthly, May 1994

☆ ☆ ☆

"Texans are a special people. They are honest, hard working, loyal and patriotic. When a Texan gives his word, you can chisel it in stone. When a Texan shakes your hand on a deal, you don't need anything else."

Bill Clements
Texas Is

"Ronnie, stick with me and we'll make it 60,000."

Lyndon Baines Johnson, to *Texas Observer* publisher Ronnie Dugger,
when Dugger explained the circulation of his newspaper was 6,000
Texas Celebrates!

☆ ☆ ☆

"As governor of the Sooner State, there has always
been a warm spot in my heart for Baja Oklahoma."

Former Oklahoma Governor George Nigh commenting on his neighbor
to the south.
Texas Is

☆ ☆ ☆

"If the election was held on Southwest Airlines, I'd
win in a heartbeat."

George W. Bush, before his election as governor
Texas Monthly, May 1994

113

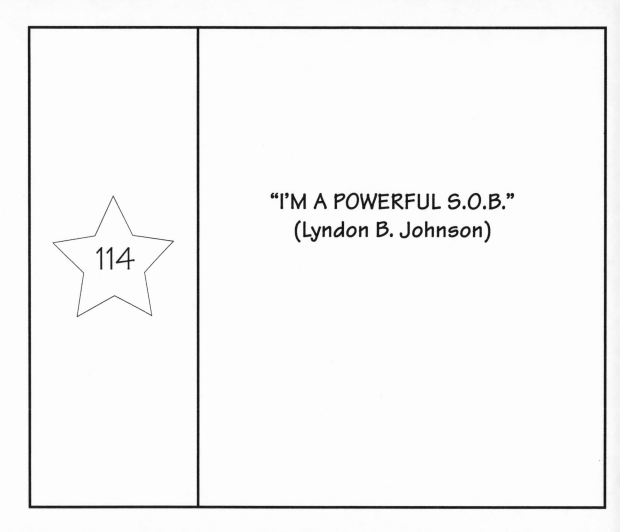

114

"I'M A POWERFUL S.O.B."
(Lyndon B. Johnson)

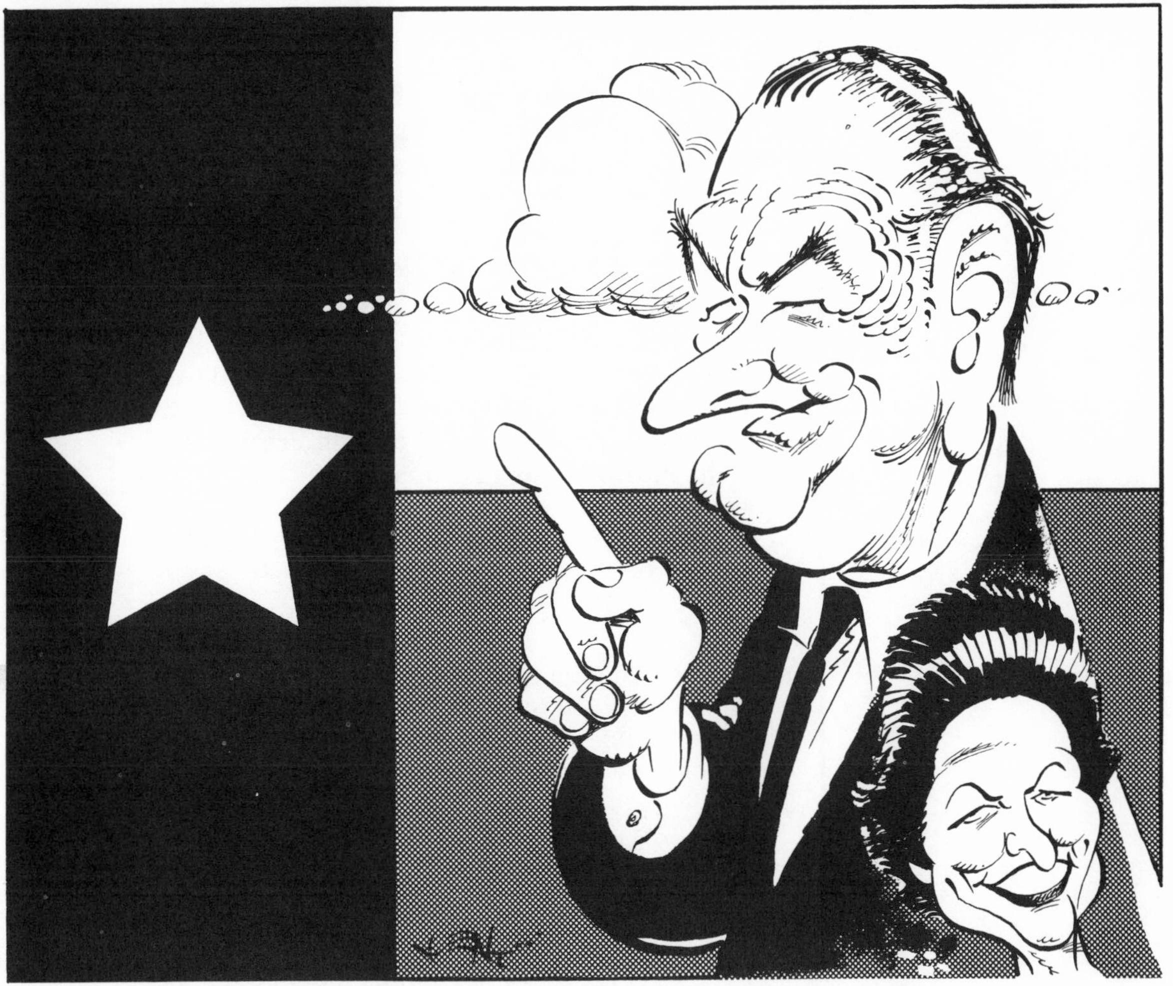

116

Throughout the history of Texas, perhaps the one man who has personified Texas politics and all that implies—was Lyndon Baines Johnson. His political career was planted and nurtured in the Texas Hill Country, and it blossomed in Washington, D.C., where President Johnson was one of the most successful political animals of our time.

While his days in the White House were filled with memorable quotes, the early Johnson days in Austin remind us of many of our current Lone Star politicians who dream of becoming President.

The most famous LBJ quote sums up the man better than a thousand pictures: "I'm a powerful S.O.B., you know that?"

☆ ☆ ☆

"This is a moment that I deeply wish my parents could have lived to share. In the first place, my father would have enjoyed what you so generously said of me and my mother would have believed it."

Lyndon B. Johnson, during an address at Baylor University upon receipt of an honorary degree, May 28, 1965
The Johnson Wit

"Who in the hell is this boy Lyndon Johnson; where the hell did Kleberg get a boy with savvy like that?"

Cactus Jack Garner, 1934, describing Lyndon B. Johnson as a young congressional assistant to Richard Kleberg
The Years of Lyndon Johnson: The Path to Power

☆ ☆ ☆

"My definition of 'off the record' is that you don't even tell it at the Press Club Bar."

Lyndon B. Johnson
The Johnson Wit

☆ ☆ ☆

"You can't be in politics unless you can walk in a room and know in a minute who's for you and who's against you."

Sam E. Johnson's (Lyndon B. Johnson's father's) favorite saying
The Years of Lyndon Johnson: The Path to Power

117

"I want that house! Every woman wants a home of her own. I've lived out of a suitcase ever since we've been married. I have no home to look forward to. I have no children to look forward to, and I have nothing to look forward to but another election."

Lady Bird Johnson, to her husband Lyndon, in 1942, discussing the purchase of their first home, in Washington, D.C.
The Years of Lyndon Johnson: Means of Ascent

☆ ☆ ☆

"The Secretary of the Treasury is in charge of taking half your money and the Attorney General sues you for the other half."

Lyndon B. Johnson, introducing members of his cabinet in 1965
The Johnson Wit

☆ ☆ ☆

"We had a preacher back home who dropped his notes and his dog grabbed them and tore them up. And when the preacher went to the pulpit he apologized to his congregation and said, 'I am very sorry today. I have no sermon. I'll just have to speak as the Lord directs. But I'll try to do better next Sunday.'"

Lyndon B. Johnson
Don't Throw Feathers at Chickens

"Someone said that lawyers are like bread they are best when young and fresh."

Lyndon B. Johnson, 1964
The Johnson Wit

☆ ☆ ☆

"Lyndon had one of the most incredible capacities for dealing with older men. I never saw anything like it. He could follow someone's mind around, and get where it was going before the other fellow knew where it was going. I saw him talk to an older man, and the minute he changed subjects, Lyndon was there ahead of him, and saying what he wanted to hear—before he knew what he wanted to hear."

Tommy Corcoran, former Franklin Delano Roosevelt strategist, 1980
The Years of Lyndon Johnson: The Path to Power

☆ ☆ ☆

"I was beaten by a stuffed ballot box, and I can prove it."

Coke Stevenson, September 2, 1948, after final results were announced in the Senatorial election, showing him losing to Lyndon B. Johnson by eighty-seven votes
The Duke of Duval

119

"I am aware that by many persons, it is considered in the nature of a joke to become a candidate and to be elected as a member of the Legislature."

Sam E. Johnson, 1904
The Years of Lyndon Johnson: The Path to Power

☆ ☆ ☆

"I wish you could have seen Billy Graham and Bill Moyers in that [White House] pool together the other day. Everyone else was already a Christian, so they just took turns baptizing each other."

Lyndon B. Johnson, on having a former preacher, Bill Moyers, as his press secretary, 1964
The Johnson Wit

☆ ☆ ☆

"The women liked her. Every woman sympathized with her. If they didn't like her for herself—and they did—they liked her because they saw what she had to put up with. It made what they had to put up with not so bad."

Nellie Connally, wife of John Connally, on Lady Bird Johnson's life, in 1941
Means of Ascent

120

"We proved in the West Virginia primary that Protestants will vote for a Catholic."

Lyndon B. Johnson, July 13, 1960
The Johnson Wit

☆ ☆ ☆

"Adlai Stevenson encountered a staunch supporter who said, 'Governor, you are going to win because every thinking person in America is going to vote for you.' Stevenson replied, 'To win you have to have a majority.'"

Lyndon B. Johnson, on Adlai Stevenson's a campaign trail experience
Don't Throw Feathers at Chickens

☆ ☆ ☆

"Come, let us reason together."

Lyndon B. Johnson
The Johnson Wit

☆ ☆ ☆

"You see what a dog will do when he gets in a crowd of bankers?"

Lyndon B. Johnson, as he lifted his beagle by the ears and the dog yelped loudly, while a group of financial experts visited the White House
The Washington Post, April 28, 1964

121

"Go ahead with the dark blue one, wherever I am I can always use that."

Lyndon B. Johnson, in a hospital bed after suffering a heart attack in 1955, on picking out suits he had ordered
The Johnson Wit

☆ ☆ ☆

"Who the hell is Lyndon Johnson?"

Texas political strategist Claud Wild, 1937, responding to Governor Allred's suggestion that he manage Lyndon B. Johnson's first congressional campaign
The Years of Lyndon Johnson: The Path to Power

☆ ☆ ☆

"I want you to know this: that no one person, not even with Lady Bird and Linda Bird and Luci Baines to help him, can lead this nation by himself."

Lyndon B. Johnson, 1964
The Johnson Wit

☆ ☆ ☆

**Santa Anna took the Alamo—that was 1836
Sam Johnson saved the Alamo—that was 1905**
Headline in a San Antonio newspaper, 1905, after Sam E. Johnson sponsored legislation to purchase the Alamo and save it from destruction
The Years of Lyndon Johnson: The Path to Power

"I've got an economic advisor who needs an economic advisor. He's broke."

Lyndon B. Johnson, on his chief economic advisor, Dr. Walter W. Heller, who resigned in April 1964, for financial reasons
The Johnson Wit

☆ ☆ ☆

"The fact that a man is a newspaper reporter is evidence of some flaw of character."

Lyndon B. Johnson
Don't Throw Feathers at Chickens

☆ ☆ ☆

"I've just met the most remarkable young man. Now I like this boy, and you're going to help him with anything you can."

Franklin D. Roosevelt to Tommy Corcoran, 1937, after FDR had met LBJ for the first time.
The Years of Lyndon Johnson: The Path to Power

☆ ☆ ☆

"I always like small parties, and the Republican party is just about the size I like."

Lyndon B. Johnson
Don't Throw Feathers at Chickens

123

"Being President."

Lyndon B. Johnson, December 1963, at his first press conference as President, when a reporter asked him what he regarded as the biggest single problem he faced as President
The Johnson Wit

☆ ☆ ☆

"Of course, Sam E. Johnson was the best man I ever knew."

Congressman Wright Patman, 1979
The Years of Lyndon Johnson: The Path to Power

☆ ☆ ☆

"You ain't learning nothing when you're talking."

Lyndon B. Johnson
Don't Throw Feathers at Chickens

☆ ☆ ☆

"I knew he was figuring on running for office. I didn't know what office he was going to run for, but I knew he was going to run for some office, and I knew he was going to run for a big office. And I was willing to buy a ticket on him."

Ed Clark, describing his impression of Lyndon B. Johnson in 1936, when Clark was Texas Secretary of State.
The Years of Lyndon Johnson: The Path to Power

"Hyperbole was to LBJ what oxygen is to life."

Bill Moyers
Genuine Texas Handbook

☆ ☆ ☆

"He doesn't have enough sense to pour piss out of a boot with the instructions written on the heel."

Lyndon B. Johnson, on one of his aides
Don't Throw Feathers at Chickens

☆ ☆ ☆

"The guy's just got extra glands."

Interior Department official Abe Fortas describing Lyndon B. Johnson, 1937
The Years of Lyndon Johnson: The Path to Power

☆ ☆ ☆

"No, I was born in a manger."

Lyndon B. Johnson to German Premier Ludwig Erhard, who had asked Johnson if he was really born in a log cabin
Don't Throw Feathers at Chickens

125

"I had never seen such a big turkey. I didn't have anything big enough to cook it in."

Constituent's description of present from young Congressman
Lyndon B. Johnson, 1937
The Years of Lyndon Johnson: The Path to Power

☆ ☆ ☆

"Until justice is blind to color, until education is unaware of race, until opportunity is unconcerned with the color of men's skins, emancipation will be a proclamation but not a fact."

Lyndon B. Johnson
The Best of Texas

☆ ☆ ☆

"Next time you need a dam in Idaho, you just go ask Walter Lippmann."

Lyndon B. Johnson to Vietnam dove Senator Frank Church, who had just responded that his ideas on Vietnam came from Walter Lippmann
Too Funny To Be President

"He was many things: proud, sensitive, impulsive, flamboyant, sentimental, earthy, mean at times, bold, euphoric, insecure, magnanimous, the best dancer in the White House since Washington, but temperamental, melancholy, and strangely ill at ease, as well. He had an animal sense of weakness in other men, on whom he could inflict a hundred cuts."

Bill Moyers, on Lyndon B. Johnson
LBJ: The White House Years

☆ ☆ ☆

"A long time ago I learned that telling a man to go to hell and making him go are two different propositions."

Lyndon B. Johnson
Don't Throw Feathers at Chickens

☆ ☆ ☆

"I never saw anyone campaign as hard as that. I never thought it was *possible* for anyone to work that hard."

Ed Clark, describing Lyndon B. Johnson's 1937 congressional campaign
The Years of Lyndon Johnson: The Path to Power

127

"Well, the governor of Texas does not know that I am in the (Texas State) Senate, but the president of the United States knows it."

Barbara Jordan, on an invitation by President Lyndon B. Johnson to meet with him in the White House shortly after she was elected the first black woman state senator in Texas, in 1967
LBJ: The White House Years

☆ ☆ ☆

"He [Lyndon Johnson] may have been a son of a bitch, but he was a colossal son of a bitch."

Former LBJ Press Secretary George Reedy
Lyndon B. Johnson: A Memoir

☆ ☆ ☆

"There are no favorites in my office. I treat them all with the same general inconsideration."

Lyndon B. Johnson, on his staff
Don't Throw Feathers at Chickens

128

"Franklin D., Lyndon B., and Jesus C."

Irreverent pressroom version of Congressional candidate Lyndon B.
Johnson's campaign slogan, "Franklin D. and Lyndon B.," 1937
The Years of Lyndon Johnson: The Path to Power

☆ ☆ ☆

"The first lady is, and always has been, an unpaid
public servant elected by one person, her husband."

Lady Bird Johnson
The Best of Texas

☆ ☆ ☆

"Lyndon was sometimes his own worst enemy. . . .
He was an exciting person to live with, and I
consider myself very lucky. I know we were better
together than we were apart."

Lady Bird Johnson, after the death of Lyndon B. Johnson
LBJ: The White House Years

129

"There is something different about this country from any other part of the nation. The climate is generally pleasant, the sun generally bright, the air seems to be always clean, and the water is pure. The moons are a little fuller here, the stars are a little brighter, and I don't know how to describe the feeling other than, I guess, we all search at times for serenity, and it's serene here. And there's something about this section that brings new life, and new hope, and a really balanced and better viewpoint after you've been here a few days."

Lyndon B. Johnson, 1972, on his native state
Power, Money and the People

☆ ☆ ☆

"I don't think Lyndon was either a conservative or a liberal. I think he was whatever he felt like he needed to be. Winning is the name of the game. I have no doubt that he could have become either an ultra-liberal or ultra-conservative, if that would have brought a victory. Now that suggests hypocrisy, doesn't it? But, well—winning is the name of the game. Lyndon was a trimmer, he would be guided by no philosophy or ideals. He would trim his sails to every win."

Former Lyndon B. Johnson assistant L.E. Jones, 1979
The Years of Lyndon Johnson: The Path to Power

"I wasn't addressing you, Mr. President."

Bill Moyers, who was saying grace at a presidential lunch when Lyndon
B. Johnson snapped. "Speak up, Bill! I can't hear a damn thing."
Don't Throw Feathers at Chickens

☆ ☆ ☆

"I'm a powerful S.O.B., you know that?"

Lyndon B. Johnson
Genuine Texas Handbook

131

132

"THOSE THIRTY DIRTY
BASTARDS."
(1970-'80s)

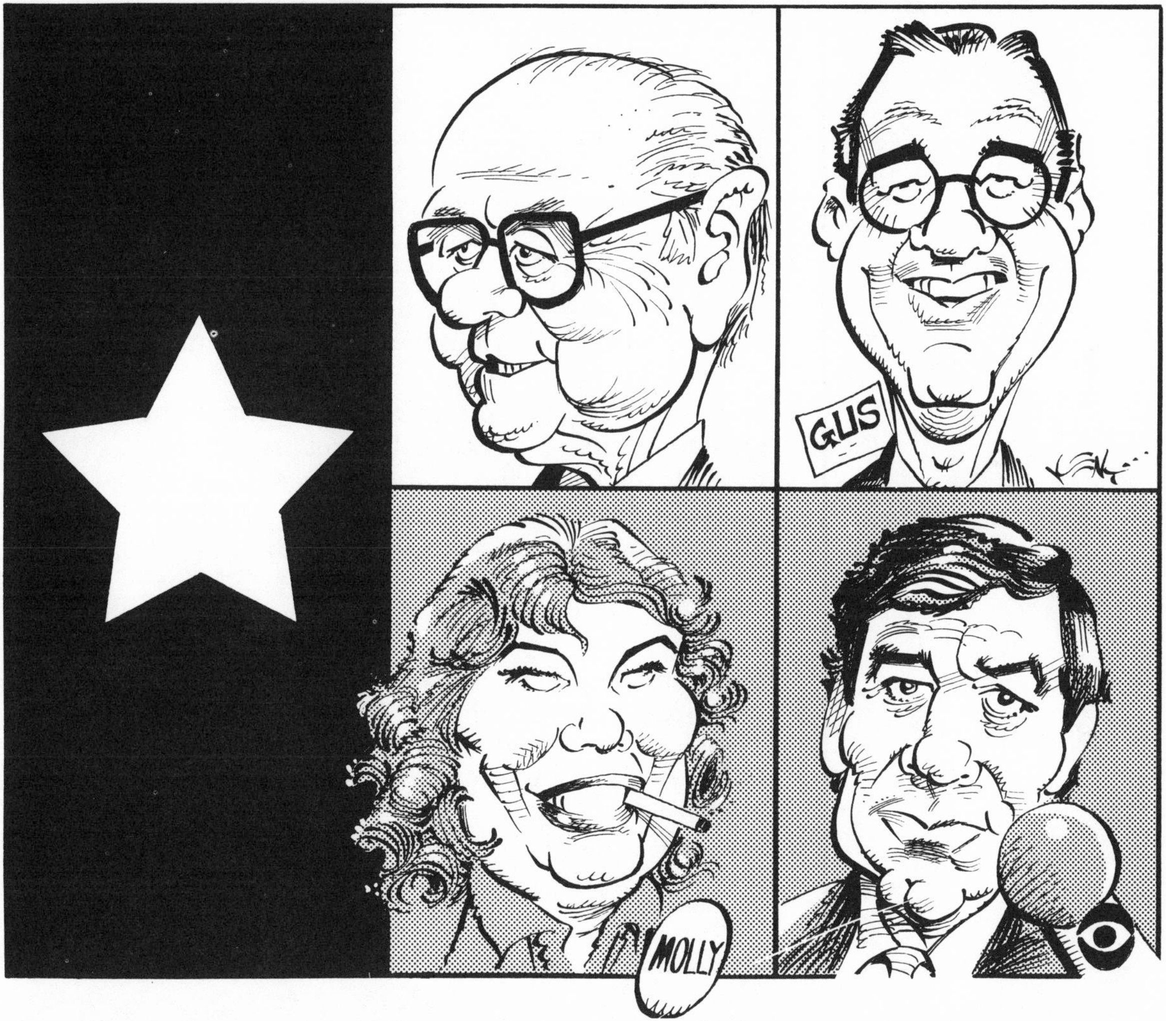
GUS
MOLLY

134

The early Seventies brought one of the greatest political scandals in Texas political history, the Sharpstown Bank scandal. Most major Texas politicians became ex-politicians during this era. Led by Frances "Sissy" Farenthold, the so-called "Dirty Thirty" helped turn Austin upside down. The Dirty Thirty was a group of liberal and loyalist legislators in the Texas House. House Speaker Gus Mutscher (who became one of those "exes," along with Governor Preston Smith and other high-ranking officials) summed up the feelings of his followers towards the Dirty Thirty who opposed him when he muttered those famous fighting words on March 15, 1971, "Those bastards—those thirty dirty bastards."

☆ ☆ ☆

"I remember once looking back at Earth [from the moon] and started to think, 'Gee that's beautiful.' Then I said to myself, 'Quit screwing off and go collect rocks.' We figured reflection wasn't productive."

Astronaut (and native Texan) Alan L. Bean
The Best of Texas

"Oh, yes, I've heard of him. He's a damn good judge and I'd like to appoint him. But do you think he can come up with ten thousand dollars or so for my next campaign?"

Governor Preston Smith, circa 1970
Shadow on the Alamo

☆ ☆ ☆

"Performing doesn't turn me on. It's an egomaniac business, filled with prima donnas—including this one."

Network anchorman (and former Houston TV reporter) Dan Rather
The Best of Texas

☆ ☆ ☆

"When a man runs for office, he ought to expect the roof to fall in on him."

Oilman Charles Ford, 1970
Shadow on the Alamo

135

136

"The only pollution we have in our country is sandstorms."

Bill Heatley, chairman, Texas House of Appropriations Committee, 1970
Shadow on the Alamo

☆ ☆ ☆

"Martin Dies named more names in one single year than Joe McCarthy did in a lifetime."

Robert Griffith, historian, on former Texas Congressman and Chairman of the House Un-American Activities Committee Martin Dies
The Politics of Fear, 1970

☆ ☆ ☆

"That's one of the main problems with Bill Heatley. He's gotten away with so many ridiculous things that if he ever goes crazy or becomes senile no one will know it. This is probably the only place in the world where 180 elected officials can kiss the ass of a maniac and never realize it."

Description of Bill Heatley, Texas House Appropriations Committee, by anonymous fellow legislator, 1971
Shadow on the Alamo

"Whereas, the Capitol building is not the property of the governor, lieutenant governor, nor the Speaker of the Texas House of Representatives, but rather it belongs to all the people of our great state; and Whereas, no governor, lieutenant governor, Speaker of Texas House of Representatives has ever had any room in the Capitol dedicated to him during his administration; and, Whereas, it is extremely bad precedent for any room in the Capitol to be dedicated to any Speaker or any other public official during his term of service; now therefore be it Resolved, That the plaque affixed to the wall in Committee Room G-13 which reads 'Gus Mutscher Committee Room' be removed by March 1, 1971; and be it further Resolved, That the picture of Speaker Mutscher on the wall G-13 be removed and presented to the Honorable Gus Mutscher by the members of the 62nd Session of the Texas House of Representatives at the close of said session."

Texas House of Representatives Journal No. 1, February 11, 1971
Shadow on the Alamo

137

138

"Those loans were collateralized by the Office of the Speaker of the House and that office doesn't belong to Gus Mutscher. It belongs to you and me and the people of Texas."

District Attorney Bob Smith, closing argument, the conspiracy trial of Gus Mutscher, 1972

☆ ☆ ☆

"I had the Sharpstown Bank under a microscope during the last half of 1970. One of my examiners went in there almost every day. We checked every transaction. Nothing got by us. That was the best-run bank in the state from June on. And it would have stayed that way if the SEC hadn't filed that suit and started a run on the bank."

Robert Stewart, State Banking Commissioner, 1971
Shadow on the Alamo

"When they tell me that these two men [Tommy Shannon and Gus Mutscher] who work together every day and every evening did not discuss this stock transaction, I'm willing to believe them. When they tell me that these same two men happened to buy their stock on the same day with financing from the same bank without discussing this stock transaction, I'm still willing to believe them. But when they try to tell me that these very same men got into the same car and rode together for 165 miles in order to sell their stock to the same man in the same place at the same price without discussing their stock transaction, that's when I stop believing them."

Bob Vale, Texas legislator and member of the "Dirty Thirty," 1971, during the Sharpstown Bank scandal
Shadow on the Alamo

☆ ☆ ☆

"If I started worrying about how my constituents are going to react to every move I make, I wouldn't be able to do my job here. I'll do what I think is right and explain it later."

Ed Harris, Texas legislator and member of the "Dirty Thirty," 1971, during the Sharpstown Bank scandal
Shadow on the Alamo

139

140

"As we pause on this hallowed day to observe the anniversary of the Texas Declaration of Independence, let us be reminded that this great document was endorsed with the blood of those who fell at the Alamo, at Goliad, and at San Jacinto. Let us ordain, then, that the blood of all Texans, shed in the causes of freedom, shall not have been in vain. Yet the enemies of freedom are always with us— apathy, indifference, lack of understanding, and compromise of principles. When we abdicate our responsibilities, we relinquish the right to choose a course of action."

Bill Heatley, March 2, 1991, during the height of the Sharpstown banking scandal.
Shadow on the Alamo

☆ ☆ ☆

"Several measures on the calendar were the result of a great deal of time and study by Senate General Investigating Committee. As I have stated previously, these reforms in the banking laws have been long overdue."

Gus Mutscher, 1971, during the height of the Sharpstown bank scandal
Shadow on the Alamo

"Everything You Touch Turns to Dirt."

Song composed by Johnny Nelms, 1971, to entertain Gus Mutscher and
the other members of the Texas House of Representatives
Shadow on the Alamo

☆ ☆ ☆

"I'm going to get Tom Bass if it's the last thing I do.
He's been a chicken-shit from the beginning."

Gus Mutscher describing a fellow legislator, May, 1971
Shadow on the Alamo

☆ ☆ ☆

"Never quit politicking and never underestimate
your opponent."

Gus Mutscher, Speaker of the Texas House, 1971
Shadow on the Alamo

141

"The important thing to realize is that none of these guys is capable of inventing or creating anything—not an idea, not a scheme, nothing. They were just imitating what they saw around them and doing a damn rotten job of it."

Unidentified lobbyist, describing Preston Smith, Gus Mutscher, and others involved in the Sharpstown Bank scandal, 1971
Shadow on the Alamo

☆ ☆ ☆

"I don't know why public officials should be singled out for exposure."

Preston Smith, 1971, during the Sharpstown Bank scandal
Shadow on the Alamo

☆ ☆ ☆

"On growing up female in Texas; I had a choice of role models—Ma Ferguson or the Kilgore Rangerettes."

Molly Ivins
Texas Celebrates!

"I don't believe a state official should use his position to further enrich himself."

Preston Smith, 1971
Shadow on the Alamo

☆ ☆ ☆

"I've never seen another politician like him, except maybe Lyndon Johnson. Ben Barnes never makes you do what he wants. He makes you want to do what he wants."

Charles Schnabel, secretary of the Texas Senate, 1971, on Lieutenant Governor Ben Barnes
Shadow on the Alamo

☆ ☆ ☆

If only Hitler could have seen it

Headline over story of Washington, D.C. peace demonstration
The Dallas Morning News, 1971

143

"It's undoubtedly the most difficult decision we make here."

Molly Ivins, *The Texas Observer,* which periodically singles out the most inane and inept newspaper in Texas for a Joseph Pulitzer Memorial Award, 1971
Shadow on the Alamo

☆ ☆ ☆

"Surely, if you can use five million dollars of taxpayer money to exhibit old bones, you can spend one-tenth of that to save bones that are living now."

Texas legislator Lane Denton, during 1971 debate on building an archaeological museum as opposed to funding research for kidney disease.
Shadow on the Alamo

☆ ☆ ☆

"And the Defense lawyers kept saying, 'there was nothing unusual about the way the bill was passed.' And I wanted to say, 'Right, it wasn't unusual. No hearing. No debate. No one had read the thing. Just slipped through. That isn't unusual. That's the way Gus runs the House. That's what's wrong!'"

Molly Ivins, describing the 1972, Gus Mutscher conspiracy trial
The Texas Observer

144

"To me the recurrent theme in the trial was being seized by a ridiculous desire to leap to my feet and explain the House of Representatives to the jury. 'Do you believe,' a defense lawyer inquired with insidious persuasiveness, 'that 123 legislators would have voted for this bill if they didn't think it was a good idea?' And I wanted to jump and say, 'Yes, yes, of course they would, that's the way it works!'"

Molly Ivins, describing the 1972, Gus Mutscher conspiracy trial
The Texas Observer

☆ ☆ ☆

"Sam Rayburn did all his serious business in pencil on the back of a used envelope."

Journalist and historian David Halberstam, 1972
The Years of Lyndon Johnson: The Path to Power

☆ ☆ ☆

"I've had so many ups and downs over the last 30 years, I've learned to live with both."

Willie Nelson
The Best of Texas

145

146

"I spent ten years working in Congress. I met some good people there, some hard-working people, but by and large most congressman and senators are interested in themselves. Too many of them, whether they are liberals or conservatives, get interested in the perks of office, the privileges. They'd like to be called 'your excellency' and wear robes and crowns, I guess."

Larry L. King, 1980
Talking With Texas Writers

☆ ☆ ☆

"The difference between Texas and communist Russia is, in communist Russia the government uses newspapers to tell lies, but in Texas we get to make up our own lies."

Joe Bob Briggs
Texas Is

"If El Paso were ever accepted as a part of Texas, the state would be much better off."

El Paso Mayor Jonathan Rogers, 1985
Texas Is

☆ ☆ ☆

"I'll be hanged if I'm going to be milking cows at 3 A.M. for the rest of my life. There's got to be an easier way."

Texas promoter and ex-convict Billie Sol Estes
Billie Sol, King of the Texas Wheeler-Dealers

147

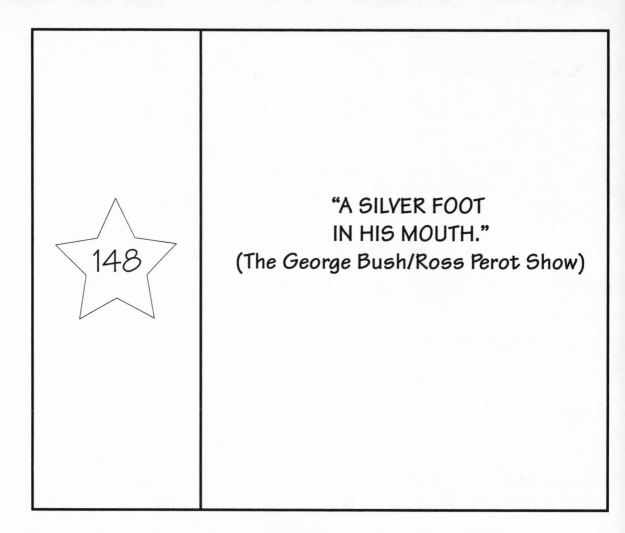

148

"A SILVER FOOT
IN HIS MOUTH."
(The George Bush/Ross Perot Show)

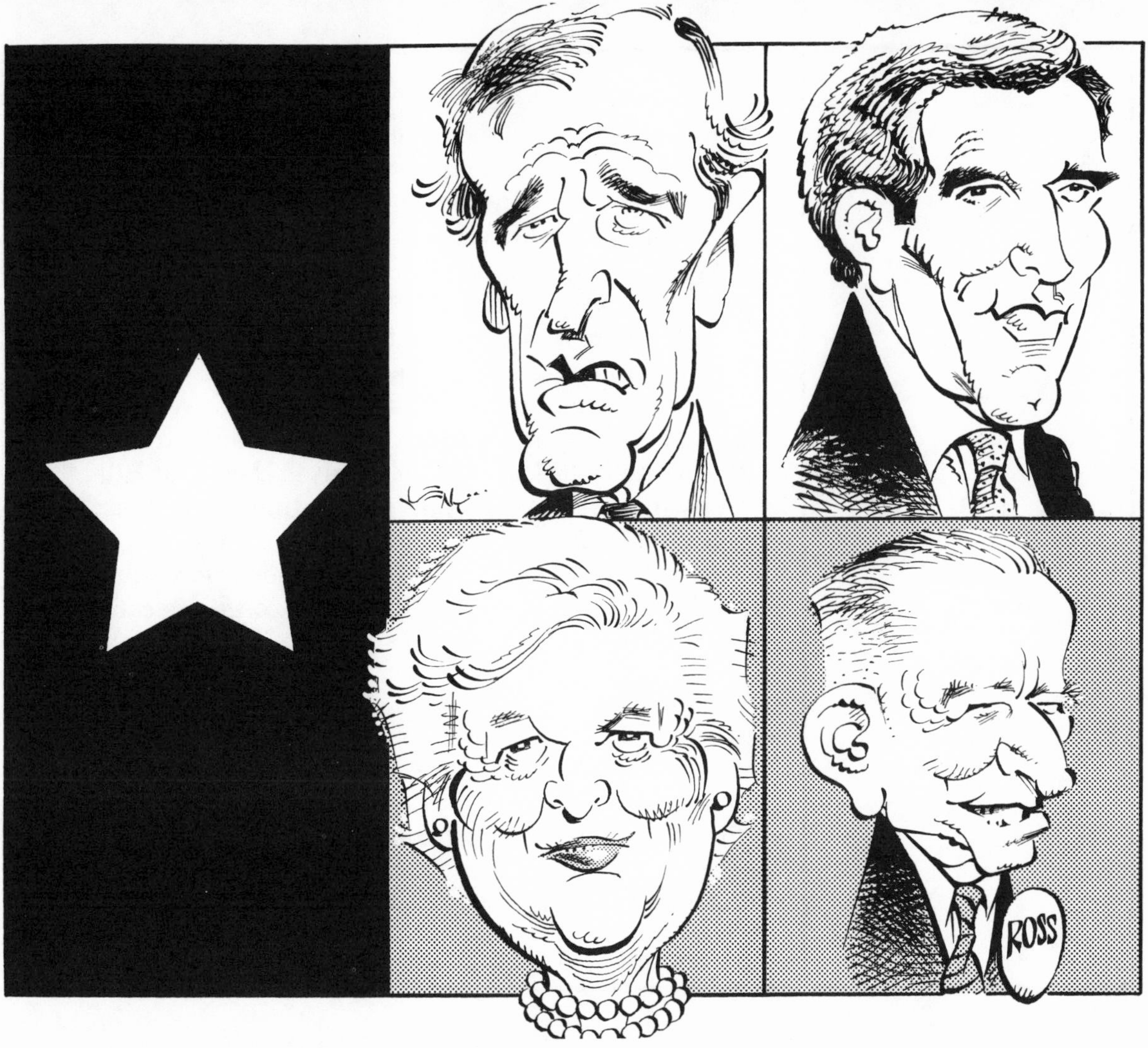
ROSS

150

After the Texas economy went down the tubes in the mid-eighties, it took about a decade to turn it back around. In the meantime, a whole army of Texans took Washington, D.C., by storm after George Bush was elected President in 1988. While Texas was riding high on the national political front, the election of '92 brought out the most unlikely antagonist to Bush's re-election—fellow Texan Ross Perot. Running as an independent, the outspoken Dallas billionaire recorded an astounding twenty percent of the national vote and knocked Bush out of the White House, allowing Arkansas Democrat Bill Clinton to step in. But that didn't sting as much as the 1988 Democratic National Convention when Texan Ann Richards spoke those famous words that Bush still hears in his sleep: "Poor George. He can't help it. He was born with a silver foot in his mouth."

☆ ☆ ☆

"Read my lips. No new taxes."

George Bush
Republican National Convention, 1988

"Calling George Bush shallow is like calling a dwarf short."

Molly Ivins
Texas Monthly, November 1992

☆ ☆ ☆

"Any man born in the United States is twice blessed. And he is thrice blessed if he is born in Texas."

Texas billionaire Ross Perot, 1979
The Establishment in Texas Politics

☆ ☆ ☆

"As if it didn't matter that school children once hid under their desks in drills to prepare for nuclear war. I saw the chance to rid our children's dreams of the nuclear nightmare, and I did. Over the past four years, more people have breathed the fresh air of freedom than in all of human history. I saw a chance to help, and I did."

George Bush
The Best of Texas

151

"How many Texans do you know whose idea of Mexican food is refried quiche?"

U.S. Senator John Glenn, on George Bush

☆ ☆ ☆

"We need to worry about how things are and how to make things better and how to fix things and how to correct mistakes we've made and to leave our children a stronger, better country so that the American dream still exists for them and they can dream great dreams and have those dreams come true."

Ross Perot
The Best of Texas

☆ ☆ ☆

"He's a toothache of a fellow."

Jim Hightower, on George Bush
Don't Throw Feathers at Chickens

"Today is Pearl Harbor Day. Forty-seven years ago today we were hit, and hit hard, at Pearl Harbor."

George Bush, speaking to an American Legion convention on September 7, 1988.
Texas Monthly, January 1989

☆ ☆ ☆

"Detroit has created a new car for George Bush. It has no seat and no steering wheel, and it's for consumers who've lost their ass and have nowhere to turn."

U.S. Senator Tom Harkin
Don't Throw Feathers at Chickens

☆ ☆ ☆

"That dog literally comes between us at night. She wedges right up between our heads and Bar likes it. She's failing with the discipline."

George Bush, on their dog, Millie
Texas Monthly, March 1989

153

154

"This happened yesterday, a beautiful experience. We expect to have puppies in the White House."

George Bush, on his dog Millie's pregnancy
Texas Monthly, March 1989

☆ ☆ ☆

"I want to shock the system so that people will talk issues."

Ross Perot
D Magazine, June 1992

☆ ☆ ☆

"So we got home last night—I say 'home'—we did. Climbed into bed. And I—nervous guy, you know, tension and work—my system working on the 6 A.M. call."

George Bush, in a typical example of "Bushspeak"
Texas Monthly, March 1989

"We could all take a lesson from the Kansas City Chiefs about competitiveness. They're having a great season. Of course, this afternoon I'll be in St. Louis saying the same thing about the Cardinals."

George Bush, speaking in Kansas City in 1991. The NFL Cardinals had moved to Phoenix by then.
Texas Monthly, January 1992

☆ ☆ ☆

"Seventy-five percent of high school seniors don't know who Whitman or Thoreau is. Twenty-five percent of college seniors in Texas can't name the country on Texas' southern border. That's scary."

Ross Perot
Texas Monthly, December 1988

☆ ☆ ☆

"It will be like turning a bunch of bulldogs loose on a bunch of poodles."

Ross Perot's assessment of EDS executives whom he thought would make the company easy prey in 1988.
Texas Monthly, December 1988

155

"I imagine the squirrels in the lawn have a budget, and I don't mean it in that context."

Ross Perot, on his analysis of the legislature's budget problems
D Magazine, January 1988

☆ ☆ ☆

"From the day I first had money I've been trying to solve problems that a lot of liberals just wring their hands about."

Ross Perot
Texas Monthly, December 1988

☆ ☆ ☆

"We certainly don't have the most able people in our society running for president. We are getting people who will endure anything because of their power drive."

Ross Perot
Texas Monthly, December 1988

"Our pioneers tamed the wilderness. Everyone said you couldn't build a transcontinental railroad, but *we* built it. Everyone said you couldn't build the Panama Canal . . . but *we* built it."

Ross Perot
Texas Monthly, December 1988

☆ ☆ ☆

"Jeez, I've never run for dogcatcher."

Ross Perot, when supporters urged him to run for president (1988)
Texas Monthly, December 1988

☆ ☆ ☆

"We've got to totally turn [Dallas] city hall around. The city council makes the General Motors board look informed."

Ross Perot, 1988
Texas Monthly, December 1988

☆ ☆ ☆

"An unguided missile."

Molly Ivins, on Ross Perot
Texas Monthly, December 1988

157

"I would disappear if they [the Bush administration] would start taking action and quit talking."

Ross Perot on CBS *This Morning* 1992

☆ ☆ ☆

"I can't tell you how many times somebody told me, 'You're the best qualified candidate. It's a shame you're not going to win.' I'd tell them, 'If everyone who felt that way would vote for me, I might win.' But they thought they would just be throwing away their vote."

Ross Perot
Texas Monthly, June 1992

☆ ☆ ☆

"[That's] about as meaningful as a million phone calls proposing Vanessa Redgrave be named Queen of England."

William F. Buckley's reaction to the deluge of phone calls to presidential candidate Ross Perot's phone banks
Texas Monthly, June 1992

"If anybody has any better ideas, I'm all ears."

Ross Perot
D Magazine, January 1993

☆ ☆ ☆

"It's beyond amateurish. I wonder if they have anything positive they stand for. Hitler's propaganda minister, Goebbels, would revel in this."

Ross Perot, alleging dirty tricks by Republicans to hurt his presidential campaign
D Magazine, June 1992

☆ ☆ ☆

"He resembles his mother, and thank heavens for that."

Ross Perot, on Ross Perot, Jr.
Texas Monthly, September 1994

☆ ☆ ☆

"He and I have so many separate projects going that we often find out by reading in the newspaper what each other is doing."

Ross Perot, Jr., on his father, Ross Perot
Texas Monthly, September 1994

160

"We could be in trouble."

George W. Bush, to his father, President Bush, when George W. looked
out the window of his North Dallas office and saw a kid selling hundreds
of "Ross Perot for President" T-shirts
Texas Monthly, May 1994

☆ ☆ ☆

"[George W.] was a wonderful, incorrigible child, who
spent many afternoons sitting in his room, waiting
for his father to come home to speak to him about his
latest transgression."

Barbara Bush, on her eldest son's childhood
Texas Monthly, May 1994

☆ ☆ ☆

"If you're a Bush, you're going to get politically
attacked just because of who you are. Damn right it
makes me more defensive of the Bush name and
more loyal to it."

George W. Bush
Texas Monthly, May 1994

"[Ross] Perot is a man who has extinguished himself in many fields."

Gib Lewis
Mark McCulloch

☆ ☆ ☆

Ross Perot: "a man with a mind half-inch wide."

Molly Ivins
Texas Monthly, November 1992

☆ ☆ ☆

"People think we had ponderous political discussions at the dinner table. Hell, our family dinners consisted of arguments about sports."

George W. Bush, on his family life while growing up
Texas Monthly, May 1994

161

SOURCES AND FURTHER READING

Bennett, Patrick. *Talking With Texas Writers*. College Station: Texas A&M University Press, 1980.

Brann, William Cowper. *The Iconoclast*. Austin: University of Texas Press, 1935.

Briggs. Joe Bob. *A Guide to Western Civilization, or My Story*. New York: Delacorte Press, 1988.

Buenger, Walter. *Seccession and the Union in Texas*. Austin: University of Texas Press, 1984.

Carleton, Don E. *Red Scare!* Austin: Texas Monthy Press, 1985.

Caro, Robert. *The Years of Lyndon Johnson: Means of Ascent*. New York: Alfred A. Knopf, Inc., 1990.

Caro, Robert. *The Years of Lyndon Johnson: The Path to Power*. New York: Alfred A. Knopf, Inc., 1982.

Deaton, Charles. *The Year They Threw the Rascals Out*. Austin: Shoal Creek Publisher, Inc., 1973.

Dingus, Anne. *The Book of Texas Lists*. Austin: Texas Monthly Press, 1982.

Dooley, Kirk. *Everything You Ever Wanted to Know About Texas*. Dallas: Half Court Press, 1986.

Dooley, Kirk. *Hidden Dallas*. Dallas: Taylor Publishing Company, 1988.

Dooley, Kirk. *The Book of Texas Bests*. Dallas: Taylor Publishing Company, 1988.

Dugger, Ronnie. *Our Invaded Universities*. New York: W. W. Dutton and Company, Inc., 1974.

Fehrenbach, T. R. *Lone Star: A History of Texas and the Texans*. New York: The MacMillan Company, 1968.

Friend, Llerena B. *Sam Houston, the Great Designer*. Austin: UT Press, 1954.

Green, George Norris. *The Establishment in Texas Politics*. London: Greenwood Press, 1979.

163

164

Griffith, Robert. *The Politics of Fear: Joseph R. McCarthy and The Senate.* Lexington: The University Press of Kentucky, 1970.

Henderson, Richard. *Maury Maverick: A Political Biography.* Austin: UT Press, 1970.

Herring, Charles, Jr. and Walter Richter. *Don't Throw Feathers at Chickens.* Plano: Wordware Publishing, 1992.

Hicks, Michael. *How To Be Texan.* Austin: Texas Monthly Press, 1981.

Holmes Jon. *Texas, A Self Portrait.* New York: Bonanza Books, 1985.

Ide, Arthur Frederick. *Blantan Millions.* Irving: The Liberal Press, 1990.

Ivins, Molly. *Molly Ivins Can't Say That, Can She?* New York: Random House, 1991.

Jones, Eugene W., Joe E. Ericson, Lyle C. Brown and Robert S. Trotter, Jr. *Practicing Texas Politics.* Boston: Houghton Mifflin Company, 1977.

Katz, Harvey. *Shadow on the Alamo.* New York: Doubleday and Company, Inc., 1972.

Kent, Rosemary. *Genuine Texas Handbook.* New York: Workman Publishing, 1981.

Leighton, Frances Spatz. *The Johnson Wit.* New York: The Citadel Press, 1965.

Lynch, Dudley. *The Duke of Duval.* Waco: Texian Press, 1976.

Moyers, Bill and Harry Middleton. *LBJ: The White House Years.* New York: H.N. Abrams, Inc., 1990.

Orum, Anthony M. *Power, Money, & the People.* Austin: Texas Monthly Press, 1987.

Pryor, Cactus. *Inside Texas.* Bryan: Shoal Creek Publishers, Inc., 1982.

Texas Celebrates! The First 150 Years. Dallas: Southwest Media Corporation, 1986.

The Texas Almanac. Dallas: *The Dallas Morning News,* 1994.

Tolbert, Frank X. *An Informal History of Texas.* New York: Harper Brothers; Publishers, 1961.

Udall, Morris K. *Too Funny To Be President.* New York: Henry Holt & Co., 1988.

Wiener, Lynton C. and Joan. *The Best of Texas.* White Plains, NY: Peter Pauper Press, Inc., 1993.

165

INDEX

A

B

C

Caperton, Kent, 71
Caro, Robert, 5
Carpenter, Liz, 11, 98
Catlin, Wynn, 8
Cavazos, Eddie, 69
Cavazos, Lauro, 54
Chiles, Eddie, 106
Church, Frank, 126
Clark, Ed, 45, 124, 127
Clark, Ramsey, 54
Clark, Tom, 53
Clary, Alla , 46
Clayton, Billy, 24, 79
Clements, William P., Jr. (Bill), 85, 99 - 101, 112
Clinton, Bill, 150
Coke, Richard, 95
Connally, John, 97 - 98, 110
Connally, Nellie, 110, 120
Copeland, Harlon, 16
Corcoran, Tommy, 119, 123
Counts, David, 83
Creighton, Tom, 95
Crockett, Davy, 29
Crouch, Hondo, 10
Cullen, Hugh Roy, 41

D

Damron, Allan, 10
Daniels, Price, 43
Davis, E. J., 95
de la Garza, Kiki, 61
de Vaca, Cabeza, 29
Democrat, 14, 20, 150
Democratic, 16, 20, 39, 47, 67, 72, 92, 103
Democratic National Committee, 61
Democratic National Convention, 150
Denton, Lane, 144
DeVore, Jack, 59
Dies, Martin, 136
Dobie, J. Frank, 40
Doggett, Lloyd, 18, 66, 100
Downey, Morton, Jr., 19
Doyle, Theresa, 12
Driskill Hotel, Austin, 4
Dugger, Ronnie, 85, 113
Duke, David, 17

E

Earle, Ronnie, 22
Eckhardt, Bob, 60
Edwards, Chet, 82, 151
Eggers, Paul, 102

Eisenhower, Dwight D., 44, 52, 55
El Paso, 71, 147
Elkins, James A., 44
Erath, George, 31
Erhard, Ludwig, 125
Estes, Billie Sol, 147
Evans, Tim, 13

F

Farabee, Ray, 6
Farenthold, Frances "Sissy," 134
Farley, Jim, 36
Faulk, John Henry, 7, 47
Ferber, Edna, 44
Ferguson, James "Pa," 93, 95
Ferguson, Miriam A. "Ma", 93, 94, 96, 142
Ford, Charles, 135
Fortas, Abe, 125
Frank, Morris, 98
Fry, Homer, 38

G

Galbraith, John Kenneth, 12
Garner, John Nance "Cactus Jack," 52, 117
George, Tex, 39
Getty, J. Paul, 37
Glenn, John, 152
Gonzalez, Henry B., 43

Gore, Charles, 76
Goynes, Bill, 22
Graham, Billy, 120
Gramm, Phil, 10, 55
Grant, Ulysses S., 95
Greene, A. C., 5, 46
Griffith, Robert, 136
Guerrero, Lena, 68
Gunther, John, 18

H

Hagman, Larry, 19
Haig, Alexander, 62
Halberstam, David, 145
Hall, John, 85
Harkin, Tom, 153
Harris, Ed, 139
Hay, Jess, 8
Heatley, Bill, 136, 140
Heller, Walter W., 123
Henderson, Richard, 42
Henry, O., 33
Hensley, Gordon, 105
Hightower, Jim, 13, 17, 59, 66, 72, 78 - 79, 81,
    100 - 101, 152
Hill, Fred, 79
Hitler, 143, 159
Hitzges, Norm, 109
Hobby, Bill, 75 - 76, 81

Luce, Tom, 108
Luckenbach, 10

M

Marcos, Ferdinand, 57
Margaret, Texas, 94
Marshall, John, 77
Martin, Ed, 67
Martin, Mike, 80, 88
Mattox, Jim, 17, 72, 103
Mauro, Garry, 73, 100
Maverick, Maury, Jr., 9, 36, 42
Maverick, Maury, Sr., 11
Mayes, Charlotte, 6
Mayflower Madam, 20
McCain, John, 56
McCarthy, Glenn, 23
McCarthy, Joseph, 41 - 43, 53, 136
McClure, Fred, 111
McDonald, Nancy, 76
Mencken, H. L., 40
Miller, Bill, 12
Millie, 153 - 154
Molberg, Ken, 20
Montgomery, Robert, 39
Moore, Bill, 83
Mosbacher, Diane, 16
Mosbacher, Georgette, 58

Mosbacher, Rob, 87
Mosbacher, Robert, 16, 56
Moyers, Bill, 16, 19, 120, 125, 127, 131
Murphy, Audie, 38
Mutscher, Gus, 134, 137 - 142, 144 - 145
Myer, Sewall, 37

N

Nagy, Joe, 74, 149
Nelms, Johnny, 141
Nelson, Willie, 14, 145
Night, George, 113
Nixon, Richard, 98
Norris, Chuck, 21

O

O'Connor, Sandra Day, 71
O'Daniel, William Lee "Pappy," 97
Odessa, 15, 148
Oklahoma, 4, 113
Otwell, W. N., 17, 72

P

Parker, Carl, 66, 70, 75, 81, 86, 89
Parker, Jim, 69
Parmer, Hugh, 10
Patman, Wright, 124

Q

R

S

T

V

W

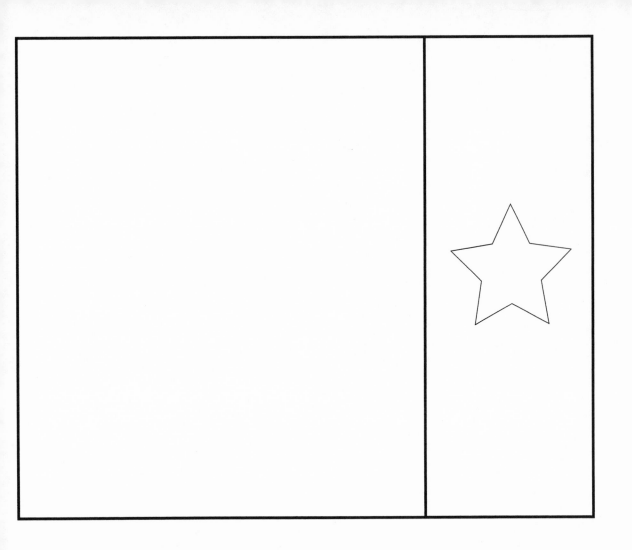

Order Form ☆ Classic Texas Quotes Series

☆ "Read my lips"
Classic Texas Political Quotes
Kirk Dooley and Eben Price
ISBN 0-89672-350-X $12.95

☆ "... 'till the fat lady sings"
Classic Texas Sports Quotes
Alan Burton
ISBN 0-89672-339-2 $9.95

Title   Quantity   Amount
_____   _____   _____
_____   _____   _____
_____   Subtotal _____
Send to:
Texas Tech University Press   Tax (TX residents
P. O. Box 41037   add sales tax) _____
Lubbock, TX 79409-1037 USA Shipping ($1.75 per book) _____
Fax: (806) 742-2979   Total _____
Toll-free: 1-800-832-4042
E-mail: prett@ttacs.ttu.edu   RLOF
Name: _____ Phone: _____
Mailing Address: _____
❑ Check or money order enclosed ❑ VISA ❑ Discover ❑ Mastercard
Account # _____ Exp. Date _____
Signature _____

Also available from Texas Tech University Press
the first book in the series

Classic Texas Quotes

"...'til the fat lady sings"
Classic Texas Sports Quotes

Alan Burton

"He's too skinny, too weak."
University of Texas baseball coach Bibb Falk, on why he didn't recruit Alvin High School pitcher Nolan Ryan, early 1960s

☆ ☆ ☆

"We're short but we're also slow and very young."
Texas A&M University basketball coach Tony Barone, assessing his team, 1991–92

ISBN 8-89672-339-9 $9.95
1-800-832-4042